PASTORING

New Testament Principles
for Pastoring
Independent Baptist Churches

David Henry Sorenson

☆
Northstar Ministries
Duluth, Minnesota

*In honor of my godly father,
Henry Charles Sorenson*

© 1998
by Northstar Ministries
1315 South Arlington Avenue
Duluth, MN 55811

For additional copies call 218-726-0209

All rights reserved
Printed in the United States of America

ISBN: 1-57502-904-9

2nd Edition 1999

Printed in the USA by

3212 East Highway 30 • Kearney, NE 68847 • 1-800-650-7888

Acknowledgments

I will be eternally grateful for my godly father, Dr. Henry C. Sorenson, whose godly life, and ministry have formed the basis for this volume. He, along with my dear mother, Viola, have given me a direct link to a godly ancestry. My father and grandfather, Dr. O. P. Lovik, pastored fundamental Baptist churches collectively for more than 100 years. That lineage has provided a rich birthright which has formed the backdrop for this book. Truly, God has given to me, my brother, and sister the heritage of them that fear His name (Psalm 61:5).

I would also like to thank my dear wife, Pam, and my sister, Mrs. Ellyn Luther, as well as my daughter, Heather, who all have helped in the proof reading and editing. Their assistance has been invaluable.

Dr. Dell Johnson of Pensacola Theological Seminary has also provided helpful comments in the final editing of this work for which I am grateful.

Finally, I would like to thank the officers and people of Northstar Baptist Church who have given me the opportunity to write this work. They are wonderful, godly people indeed.

Table of Contents

	Page
Introduction	1
Chapter One - God Gave Pastors	5
Chapter Two - Shepherd the Flock!	21
Chapter Three - Love the People!	41
Chapter Four - Help the People!	61
Chapter Five - Preach the Word!	77
Chapter Six - Do the Work of an Evangelist!	99
Chapter Seven - Take the Oversight Thereof!	115
Chapter Eight - Study to Shew Thyself Approved!	135
Chapter Nine - Pray Without Ceasing!	153
Chapter Ten - A Servant's Heart	175
Chapter Eleven - Flies in the Ointment	185
Chapter Twelve - Three Final Commands	207
Appendix	225

Introduction
(To be read)

On March 22, 1996, my father, Dr. Henry C. Sorenson, entered the courts of glory. Two funeral services were held in his memory. One was at Northstar Baptist Church in Duluth, Minnesota, where he served in retirement as an assistant pastor. The other funeral was at Faith Baptist Church in Pekin, Illinois, where he had pastored over thirty-one years. During those years, that church grew to be a work of more than one thousand people. At both memorial services, I made the comment, "Dad was a preacher. But more than that, he was a pastor." He spent over fifty-five years in the pastoral ministry. He was a pastor's pastor. During his years in the pastorate, more than sixty young men went out into the ministry, and most are still in the ministry today. They all looked to him as their pastor. (A similar number of young women entered Christian service as well.) He may not have been one of the famous pulpiteers of the land. However, he was one of the great pastors of his day.

There were many men who influenced his life and ministry. However, no one probably had more influence upon him than his father-in-law (my grandfather), Dr. Olaf P. Lovik of Wisconsin. "Grandpa" pastored for approximately 50 years. He was a mentor and guide to my father. Dr. Lovik was a Norwegian immigrant who came to these shores shortly after the turn of the 20th century. His lineage in the "old country" included preachers from some of the earliest roots of the Baptist movement in Scandinavia. There were several generations of preachers in his heritage which preceded him.

As a fundamental Baptist preacher and pastor, I have been blessed to have a direct heritage of approximately 100 years of

The Art of Pastoring

pastoring in my father and grandfather. Dad, and to a lesser degree Grandpa Lovik, taught me many nuances and keys to this blessed office. As many young men, I did not particularly appreciate their counsel in my youth. However, now that both of them are gone, I realize how much of an influence they had upon my ministry. After his death, so much of what he taught me has risen to the surface. Some of it was direct counsel and advice as he noticed rough spots in my early ministry. Other influences were simply by the example how he fulfilled his ministry.

As a young man, I made many mistakes in the ministry. I thought I had the answers. Not only had I graduated from a good Bible college and seminary, but I had also attended some of the "super" conferences and "how-to" seminars which were popular in the 1970's and 80's. I had the privilege of working together with my father for ten years as his associate at the Faith Baptist Church in Pekin, Illinois. However, as I later became a senior pastor and on my own, Dad suddenly became much smarter. His way of pastoring often was better than his young, ambitious son's way. It seemed the older I got, the smarter he became.

It took some years for the wisdom and example of my father's long tenure as a pastor to soak in. However, as I look back over his ministry and what he taught me, I believe he understood (and I to a lesser degree have come to understand) some of the major keys of pastoring. The essence of this book hopefully will reveal some of those keys.

Most veteran pastors no doubt will already understand these things. They have learned them through years of experience and the "school of hard-knocks." I would hope this volume might be of help for young pastors and those preparing for the ministry.

For over twenty-eight years in the ministry, I have observed many fellow pastors as one of their colleagues. With more than a quarter-century of perspective, I have noticed trends in ministries which seem to fit a pattern. For example, I have witnessed numerous fellows who over the years have received a strong academic education in preparation for the pastorate. Yet for some reason, they seem to struggle as pastors. I have known others who are obviously talented. However, like the old Chinese proverb, they went up like a rocket and came down like a stick. Some have been able administrators. Some have been excellent scholars able to produce fine sermons. Some have had great skills of oratory and are excellent pulpiteers. Some have a knack for promotion. Some are skilled soul winners. Others rose to positions of leadership in church associations or pastors' fellowships. Yet for some reason, some of these same men had trouble in their churches. Somehow their education, skills of homiletics, sermon delivery, church administration, or promotion over the long run do not impress their people.

The truth is, preaching and local-church program management, though necessary, really are of secondary importance to pastoring. All pastors will preach. But not all preachers pastor (though they may hold that title). All modern pastors will to one degree or another administer the affairs of their church. But being a successful administrator has little to do with the scriptural office of pastoring. Most pastors, to one degree or another, will be involved in promoting the ministry of their church. However, being a good promoter has little to do with being a pastor.

Conversely, I have known some pastors who did not have a particularly strong educational background in preparing for the ministry. Yet, their pastoral ministries have greatly flourished. This author certainly believes in young men receiving as much formal training for the ministry as possible while they can get it. However, I have witnessed men who lacked such training who have been quite successful as pastors. I have known others who were very average in their ability to organize and deliver a sermon. Yet, they have had long-term, happy pastorates. Others have had a lack of administrative ability. Yet, their people loved them as their pastor.

It seems in so many fundamental institutions in this generation, the focus is upon two areas: (1) to train young men to **preach**, including all the necessary education for good exegesis, homiletics, and pulpit delivery. Without a question this is necessary and of utmost importance. To a lesser degree another area of focus seems to be (2) training young men in local church **program management**, including church administration, program promotion, and all of the various "programs" with which local churches are involved. Again, all of this is vital and important. I would not suggest anything less.

However, it is the view of this author how men young in the ministry or preparing for the ministry need to be trained in a third area. That is (3) how to **pastor people**. Without a question, it is crucial for a pastor to be skilled in preaching and in the program management of a local church. However, if he does not pastor his people, his ministry will neither be happy or long in one place.

My father knew how to pastor people. In some measure, he shared those skills with me. In perhaps a greater measure, I simply learned from his example having grown up in his home and his influence for almost fifty years. To my regret, I surely did not learn these things early. Had I, my ministry would have been helped to a far greater extent than it was.

It is the goal of this book to share the principles contained in the Scripture which pertain to pastoring people. I will illustrate those principles primarily through the life and ministry of my father, Dr. Henry C. Sorenson. He truly exemplified them. In so doing, I hope to honor him and leave a long-term legacy of his ministry. On a greater level, I desire the name of our Lord Jesus Christ, the Chief Shepherd, be glorified.

Throughout the book, various anecdotes and illustrations will be used. They have been gleaned from more than twenty-five years in the ministry. In *almost* every case, pains have been taken to obscure the identity of parties described. Details have purposefully been distorted to obscure identity. In many cases, fictitious names have been used in the anecdotes. Any similarity to a real individual is a coincidence.

Chapter One
God Gave Pastors

"And he gave some . . . pastors"

A pastor is a shepherd. The word "pastor" appears only once in the Authorized Version of the New Testament - in Ephesians 4:11. However, as we shall soon see, the *concept* appears a significant number of times. (And this is not to mention other related terms such as "bishop" or "elder.") The English word "pastor" as found in Ephesians 4:11 is translated from the Greek word which derives from the root "poimen." Literally, it means "shepherd." In the New Testament, it is translated seventeen times as "shepherd" and once as "pastor."

Years ago, a fellow in the church would refer to me in jest as the "pasture." He would greet me on Sunday morning as Pasture Sorenson. Whenever he saw me, he would refer to me in terms of "the pasture." However, his attempt to be cute via a malapropism was more accurate than I think he knew.

The word "pastor" is indeed related to the word "pasture." Both are of Latin derivation, and both refer to the broader scope of sheep, their care, and their feeding. The motif of God's people being sheep is a familiar one throughout the Bible. For example, in the twenty-third Psalm, we read, *"The LORD is my shepherd, I shall not want"* (Psalm 23:1). The psalmist later wrote, *"For he is our God; and we are the people of his pasture, and the sheep of his hand,"* (Psalm 95:7). He further wrote in Psalm 100:3, *"We are his people, and the sheep of his pasture."*

In Matthew 9:36, it is noted how Jesus in viewing Israel of His day commented, they *"were scattered abroad as sheep, having no shepherd."* Later, John would quote Jesus saying, *"I am the door of the sheep,"* (John 10:7). In the great and classic statement made shortly later, Jesus said, *"I am the good shepherd: the good shepherd giveth his life for the sheep,"* (John 10:11). In Hebrews 13:20, He is called *"that great shepherd of the sheep, through the blood of the everlasting covenant."* Peter, in alluding back to Isaiah 53:6, wrote, *"For ye were as sheep going astray; but are now returned unto the Shepherd and Bishop of your souls."*

It is clear, God views His people as sheep whether in Old Testament Israel or the New Testament church. Jesus Christ is the chief and great Shepherd. Meanwhile on this earth, He has established under-shepherds. The most common term for this leadership is called "pastor." As noted, the word literally means "shepherd."

There are several gifts of the ministry for the local church. In Ephesians 4, the Apostle Paul digressed from the greater theme of the chapter to describe an adjunct thought. He noted in verse 7 how grace is given to each of us according *"to the measure of the gift of Christ."* In verse 8, He then quoted from Psalm 68:18 to lead into the truth how God *"gave gifts unto men."* Returning to where he was going in the first place, the apostle then noted in verse 11, *"And he gave some, apostles; and some, prophets; and some, evangelists; and some, pastors and teachers."* Though Paul addressed the idea of gifts of the Holy Spirit to individuals in I Corinthians 12 - 14, here the recipients clearly are not individuals. The gifts of apostles, prophets, evangelists, pastors, and teachers would seem quite rather to be for *the church*. The ultimate recipient of these gifts are the *people* in the church. However, the greater recipient of these gifts is the body of Christ, the local church of the New Testament.

Paul, a trained lawyer, frequently wrote as one. Verses 7 through 16 of Ephesians 4 contain a total of five sentences. Needless to say, his thought development is complex. Let us therefore attempt to present a rendering of the text taking into account the immediate context as its framework.

> "And he gave *gifts unto men,* some *as* apostles, some *as* prophets, some *as* evangelists, some *as* pastors and teachers."

The flow of the preceding context is how God through Christ gave spiritual gifts unto mankind. The idea is *not* how He gave to some churches apostles, and to others prophets, and to others still, evangelists, and finally to others, pastors and teachers. Rather, the apostle is developing how God gave a number of specific, spiritual gifts to the church in general. At one time, all of these gifts were operative. Today, only the latter remain.

Pastors and teachers are separate gifts. The two terms, *pastors and teachers* are viewed by many as a dual or combined gift referring to the same individual. A case for this position can be made grammatically. (Just as strong a case can be made for the two being separate.) However strong the grammatical implication might be, the greater context of the New Testament argues against this position. In no other place is the office of a teacher used as a dual, combination office with that of pastor, elder or bishop. For example, Paul is referred to as a "teacher" on several occasions (Acts 13:1, II Timothy 2:7, 2:11). However, to our knowledge Paul was never officially a pastor as such. He notes how he was ordained a preacher, an apostle, and a teacher in II Timothy 2:7,11. Never

The Art of Pastoring

again in the various references to elders and bishops is there intimation of a dual office of pastor/teacher.

God quite evidently has called some to a ministry of teaching, whether it be within the local church as Sunday School teachers, Christian school teachers, or as Bible college professors etc. However, teaching would seem to be a gift separate from that of shepherding a flock. There is a profound difference in duties and abilities.

A Pastor is a Shepherd

A pastor shepherds a local church. Therefore, He gave the gift of pastors. As noted above, the term "pastor" literally means "shepherd." A shepherd, on the one hand, is one who cares for the needs of the sheep on an *individual* basis. On the other, a shepherd oversees the *entire flock*. Implicit in the term is both individual care as well as oversight of the overall flock.

One thing this author has noted after more than twenty-eight years in either pastoral or associate pastoral ministries is a lack of personal care for the sheep. In this day of large ministries, it would seem pastors have focused perhaps upon the greater, overall oversight of a church and drifted away from tending to the sheep on an individual basis. If there is one thing Henry Sorenson did, it was pastor his people. Though he administratively oversaw a ministry with several dozen staff members and a congregation which at one time was more than a thousand, his forté remained pastoring the people. He was a shepherd to them not only in the pulpit, but in their homes, beside hospital beds, or wherever they needed him.

It seems there has been a proliferation of ministerial specialties. Churches today have pastors who are trained and skilled in counseling. Some are skilled administrators. Many have been trained as educators. Some have focused upon being aggressive promoters. Some lean toward being scholars. Others pride themselves in the eloquence of their oratory. Some spend much time being involved with external ministries such as fellowships or associations. All of these things are good and no doubt each can be an asset in a pastoral ministry. However, the basic office is in pastoring people.

It is noteworthy how in the various gifts of the ministry mentioned in Ephesians 4:11, the Lord did not mention administrators. To be sure, a pastor must administer. But that is not where the emphasis is. There is no mention of scholars. A pastor of necessity must be a student of the Word. But that is not what the Holy Spirit noted. There is no mention made of promoting. To one degree or another, a modern pastor will be involved in promoting his church and its ministry. However, there is no mention of this in Scripture. Though a pastor certainly will preach, even preachers are not listed among the gifts given by Jesus Christ to the church. It certainly does not say, "And He gave executives."

However, the one gift given by Jesus Christ intrinsic to the local church is the office of the pastor. Evangelists come and go. The pastor is always there (or should be). Teachers have a vital role. But they are not the shepherd. That privilege and responsibility is reserved for the man occupying the exalted office of pastor.

Many good things can detract from pastoring. It has been the observation of this author how many pastors are focused on things which may be good, but have detracted them from pastoring their people. For some, it is an inordinate emphasis on scholarship. Institutions of higher learning are by their very nature academic. It seems professors tend to beget after their own kind. In looking over the catalog of a highly regarded seminary, more than 90% of their course offerings related to the degree of pastoring were academic in nature. Their catalog denoted "practical" courses, yet they comprised about 6% of the curricula required for graduation. (Most pastors who have been out in the field for several decades will understand how in practice, the ministry is perhaps 75% practical and 25% or less academic.) Nevertheless, some pastors spend the lion's share of their time in studying. To be sure, adequate

The Art of Pastoring

preparation for teaching and preaching is a necessity. But for some, it obscures the greater ministry of pastoring their people.

I have known pastors of my generation who viewed themselves as the chief executive officer (CEO) of their church. As the God-ordained overseer, to a certain extent they are correct. However, some are so busy running the 501(c)(3) not-for-profit corporation over which they preside, also known as a church, they are too busy to pastor their people. How many a church has several layers of secretaries insulating the pastor from his own people who wish to see him? Pastors are busy. However, woe be to the preacher who is too busy to take time for his own people who have a need.

Some preachers are so involved with the affairs of the Christian school they oversee, their ministry of pastoring the people to which God has fundamentally called them fades into the background. Most preachers will proclaim the principle how the church must take priority over the school. And they are right. However, in practice, they become so enmeshed in the complications of operating a Christian school within their church, the crucial matter of pastoring their people becomes secondary.

I have known other preachers who are gone almost every week for associational or fellowship meetings of one kind or another. They may be officers in these groups or they just go for the fellowship. But the simple truth is they are gone. I once had a frustrated friend complain that his pastor was gone every Monday for various and sundry associational or committee meetings. When he was back in the office on Tuesday, he was crabby from the stress of traveling to the meetings the day prior.

My father pastored his people. He was always there when his people needed him. Nothing took precedence over meeting their needs and encouraging them. His door was always ajar. Over the years, he often lamented to me how he wished he had more time to visit his own people. Though he was always there when they were sick or had other crises in their lives, he desired to make "routine" pastoral visits upon them. Whenever he sensed a member of the church was beginning to drift or had need in their lives, Dad was at their door. He would stop and visit with them, pray with them, and encourage them. Wednesday evening was the midweek service. On Saturday evening, he always held a small men's prayer meeting for the services of the Lord's day. However, on just about any other evening of the week, he would be out visiting. He of course would go see visitors to the church or people with obvious need. However, he made it a practice to make short "drop-in" visits upon people of the church. For fifty years, Henry Sorenson made countless thousands of calls upon people of his congregations just to "pastor" them. He got to know their homes and needs because he had visited with them. He already knew about their problems when they did come for counsel. He had already been to their homes - numerous times - for prayer and encouragement.

A Pastor is There

A pastor will be there when his people need him. In the early years of my ministry, I did not think much about such mundane things as showing up for anniversary celebrations or graduations. I was too busy winning the lost, building Sunday School classes, and seeking to build the church. Do not misunderstand. Those things are all important. But what I did not understand was how important it was to be present when our people had special events in their lives. My father would say to me, "You need to be there, Dave. It is important!" And he was absolutely right. Over the decades, I have learned just how important it is to be a pastor to people and to be there when they have special times. I didn't fully understand it when Dad would urge me to be there for those sort of things. Today, I realize how crucial it is. It builds a rapport with the people. I may have had the greatest sermon in the world last Sunday. However, if I have lost the rapport of my own people because I was too busy doing other things, I have undercut my own ministry.

The Art of Pastoring

My father was always there. In earlier years when hospitals routinely kept people longer than they do today, Dad tried to visit his own people *every* day they were in the hospital. If they were particularly faithful people and if their illness was critical, he would at times visit them more than once a day to have prayer with them and encourage them. One thing I learned from him was the importance of hospital visits. When people are taken to the hospital, especially unexpectedly, it is a major crisis in their lives. Whether they happen to think of their pastor at such a time is irrelevant. If their pastor found out they were taken in, he dropped what he was doing and headed for the hospital. It was one of his people. He was their pastor. He needed to be with them. On many occasions, he arrived at the hospital *before* our member had even been moved from the emergency room to a floor bed. On some occasions, he even beat the ambulance.

If my father learned one of his people was going in for surgery the next morning, he would try to arrive early and have prayer with them before they were put under. There is something quite frightening, even for a Christian, in facing anesthesia and the surgeon's scalpel - especially the first time. Dad was there. It may have meant getting to the pre-op area at 6:30 in the morning. But he was there.

Depending upon the closeness to the ministry of the one hospitalized, Dr. Sorenson on occasions spent the entire time the patient was in surgery with the family. It may have been for intermittent prayer if the case was particularly critical. It may have been to just carry on everyday conversation with the family to take their mind off their loved one behind the doors in the surgical unit. But he was there.

I can remember several occasions when a member of our church would be sent to a distant city for treatment not locally available. Dad made it a point to be there. It was one of his people. He was their pastor. They needed him. He loved them.

When an infant was born, he tried to visit the mother and infant in the hospital even if all was well. He then would later visit them in their home to have prayer with them. If someone associated with our church wound up in jail, he was there to visit them. They may have richly deserved their incarceration. However, he tried to help them. He was their pastor. When young people from our church went off to Christian colleges, he always tried to visit them at least once during their time away. And he certainly made it a point to be present for their graduation. He was their pastor.

Talent is not Pastoring

In contrast, I am aware of men in the ministry who have been quite talented. They could preach! They were eloquent! They knew how to exegete the Scripture and develop strong sermons. Yet, they did not particularly pastor their people. Others were so busy in secondary matters such as school administration, fellowship meetings, promoting one thing or another, or just being a scholar in their study, they failed to pastor their people. Notwithstanding their talent, pulpit delivery, or other achievements, they could not understand why they were having such a difficult time in the ministry. Every man who has been in a pastoral ministry for any time knows it is not easy. Legion are the number who have fallen by the wayside, dropped out, or burned out in the ministry. Pastoring one's people may not be the panacea to cure all problems in the ministry. But I will submit to you, it will *prevent* many problems.

Some Case Histories

Let us go through several "case" histories of men I have been aware of over the years who have had serious difficulty in the ministry. It is my view, their problems could have been greatly alleviated and even precluded had they adequately pastored their people. I shall deliberately change names, distort details, and add embellishments to obscure identities. But the basic stories are true.

* * *

Great preaching and administrative skill will never take the place of pastoring one's people. Pastor Skorich was a fine fellow. He had attended a good Christian college and seminary. He was a moral and ethical man. He took a good stand on crucial issues of the day. While in seminary, his professors thought he would go far in the ministry. He carried good grades, was a good student, and had a good spirit.

As a pastor, he was an excellent preacher. In hearing him preach years ago, I would always be impressed with not only the content and homiletics of his preaching, but his delivery in the pulpit. He was quite eloquent. He also was a good teacher. He knew the Word and was skilled in drawing truths from it. He was a good administrator. When he became the pastor of the church, things were ragged in that regard. But over a period of time, Pastor Skorich was able to get a firm handle on church administration and kept things on an even keel thereafter. He was a personable fellow. He usually had a smile on his face and had a quick wit. He often had a joke on his lips. Initially, the entire church thought highly of him. He was a good preacher, a good administrator, and personable.

However, after several years, the attitude in the church had changed toward their pastor. He hadn't changed. He still had good messages. Church business affairs were stable. He was still Mister Nice Guy. But the atmosphere within the church had gone from clear and sunny to overcast. Most people could not put their finger on the problem. Pastor Skorich couldn't. But something was missing. Something was not right. People were drifting away. The attendance was slipping. People who had been there for years suddenly were not there anymore.

After several more years, the outlook within the church had gone from overcast to ominous. There were no questions about his integrity, ethics, or morals. Because of the decline in attendance, offerings were down. But he had been able to make cuts in the budget which kept church finances otherwise stable. There were rumblings among some of the deacons about possibly asking the pastor to begin looking for another place. Finally, one Sunday, he announced his resignation and call to another church. There were no tears shed. Though no one at church said anything that day, there was a collective sigh of relief. There had not been harsh words or nasty business meetings. Nobody hated the pastor. But his ministry there had gone from hot to cold.

Knowing a little about that ministry, I think I understand what the problem was. Though Pastor Skorich was a good student of the Word, a good preacher, and an adequate administrator, he had failed to pastor his people. His approach to the ministry was not unlike that of an executive. He managed the ministries and programs of the church. He made hard decisions, and if it offended someone, well that was just too bad.

He rarely visited his people. If they wished to see him, he informed them from the pulpit to make an appointment through his secretary. He would not see anyone on his day off. That was *his* day. When they came in for counsel, he told them at the outset if they were not willing to follow his advice, they were wasting his time and theirs. He preached the requisite funerals of the church, but never went to visit the bereaved family prior to or after the funeral. He figured the usual condolences over the phone when arrangements were made, coupled with his call to the visitation were adequate.

He was rather sporadic in making hospital calls. It was easy to put off such visits and by the time he got there, the party often had already gone home. Of course, making such a visit on his day off was out of the question. One day, he was confronted why he had not visited someone's family member when they had been in the hospital. He replied, that was the deacons' job.

When men in the church were out of work and discouraged, Pastor Skorich never went to see them to encourage them. When there were graduation or anniversary receptions, he often did not show up. He instructed the financial officers in the church and Christian school to be hard-nosed about unpaid bills. Though it helped put the overall ministry on a better footing business-wise, he didn't seem to have sympathy for those who were struggling to make their school bills. If someone wanted to come in for prayer about a problem, if they did not have an appointment, he instructed his secretary to have them make an appointment - of course, not on his day off.

Though Pastor Skorich was a good administrator and a good preacher, he was not a good pastor. He oversaw the overall ministry, but he did not pastor the sheep individually. One by one, his people were put off by his aloof manner of ministry. He had not failed morally, doctrinally, ethically, financially, or administratively. He failed in pastoring his people. People either voted with their feet in leaving the church, or they stayed and were unhappy. It goes without saying, Pastor Skorich was discouraged, stressed, and perplexed. He knew his doctrine was right. He thought he was adequate in the pulpit. He had kept the church on an even keel financially.

Unfortunately, though he had college and post-graduate degrees for the ministry, evidently he had never been taught the crucial art of pastoring people. He knew Greek, Hebrew, systematic theology, and church administration. He was honest, moral, personable and talented. He had a strong desire to serve the Lord. He was willing to take unpopular positions for righteousness' sake. He could prepare good sermons and was an excellent pulpiteer. But for the most part, he did not pastor his people. He managed his 501(c)(3) not-for-profit corporation. But he did not pastor his people. He nearly burned out in the ministry as a result.

God Gave Pastors

* * *

Zeal and results will never take the place of pastoring one's people. Pastor Rickover had gone to a good Christian college. He graduated with a zeal for winning the lost and building a growing New Testament church. After serving for some years as an assistant pastor, he launched out in the uncharted waters of being *the* pastor of a church. He had gone to various soul-winning and church-building conferences. He became quite skilled in such practical matters as Sunday School contests, building a church bus ministry, Sunday School promotion, and church-wide soul winning programs. As a result, his church began to grow. In fact, it grew quite rapidly.

He was a good preacher. He knew how to take a text and drive it home. As invitations were given in each public preaching service, there was hardly a Sunday when there was no response. He was a good administrator, and the church kept on an even keel in its business matters. The offerings remained solid, and all bills were paid on time.

However, as Pastor Rickover continued to attend preaching conferences, he was influenced to preach at home like some of the great pulpiteers he so admired in the conferences. There, great preachers would come and fire their gospel gun. They would preach away with a vengeance in session after session. What young pastor Rickover did not seem to understand is that conference preaching is to a totally different kind of audience than those in the pew on Sunday back home. In the conferences, the crowd was mostly preachers. The bombastic and fiery preaching was intended to encourage and stir them. However, Pastor Rickover came away with the idea how he should enter his pulpit week after week and "tan the hide" of the people. There always was some sin to be preached against. There always was some unfaithfulness to be railed against.

When he wasn't scolding his people about perceived shortcomings, he would exhort them to be doing more to serve God. Therefore, a significant percentage of his messages were focused upon motivating them to be doing more of what they ought to do. Now to be sure, every New Testament pastor has an obligation to preach against sin and urge his people to do as they ought. But Pastor Rickover as a young pastor didn't seem to quite have the right balance in his preaching. When he wasn't scorching the paint about sin, he was urging his people to do more and more. There were frequent altar calls for more soul winners. There was frequent preaching about serving God in some other capacity. Now to be sure, all of this is good in a proper perspective. Young Pastor Rickover just did not intermingle such preaching with messages of encouragement, messages of blessing, or messages designed to uplift his people.

He, for the most part, had good people. They probably were not doing as much as they should in serving the Lord. But they had been faithful and stayed by the stuff when the church had gone through difficult times. At first, such fiery preaching was a novelty to them, and they enjoyed such spirited pulpiteering. But young pastor Rickover rarely sought to encourage them. He seemed oblivious to going to the pulpit for the simple purpose of blessing his people. When there should have been preaching to strengthen discouraged Christians, he kept up excoriating messages. When there should have been a little balm of Gilead, there was more Tabasco sauce from the pulpit.

Little by little, the people grew weary of such a ministry. As in the story of Pastor Skorich above, a sullenness began to develop in the church. People at first were not sure what the problem was; they just knew something was not right. The church began to grow divided. Some backed their pastor even though they knew he should be more encouraging to them. Others had had enough. They contemplated variously either leaving the church or possibly trying to force the pastor to leave. Some of the more carnal ones began to withhold their tithe hoping to force a showdown through a financial crisis. Others just backed off in giving because of dissatisfaction. Things became tight in the church treasury. As Pastor Rickover sensed the growing financial crisis, he preached all the harder at the people. Eventually, he left just before there was a church split.

Sadly, a young pastor with a great deal of zeal in serving the Lord in building his church became a casualty in the ministry. He was absolutely right in seeking to stir his church. His problem developed in that he did not pastor his people. He preached hard. He won souls. He promoted and sought to motivate his people. He worked hard, very hard. But sadly, no one had ever taught him to also be a pastor to his people. He had been stirred to build his church. But no one had ever trained him in the delicate skill of pastoring the people he already had. He left the church a broken young man. He had poured his heart and soul into that ministry. He had given it his all. He had done his best. His error was in what he did not do. He did not pastor his people. He took them for granted. He viewed them as soldiers in an army who would always be there whether they wanted to be or not. He should have viewed them as sheep who could very easily scatter, who needed a pastor to encourage, strengthen, love and help them. If he had established that foundation, he may have had more success in seeking to motivate them or occasionally scold them from the pulpit.

The term "pastor" is not by accident. Before a pastor can motivate or scold his people, he must love them, encourage them, help them, and be a friend to them. A pastor is to administer the affairs of the church. In the coming chapter, we will note other terms used in the New Testament concerning the leadership of the local church. The word "bishop" indeed denotes oversight and management. However, in Ephesians 4:11 where the apostle described the various gifts given for the ministry in the local church, he did not say, and "And he gave some, administrators." It says, "And He gave some, *pastors.*" It does not say, "And he gave some, preachers." It says, "And he gave some, *pastors.*" It does not say, "And he gave some, elders." It says, "And he gave some, *pastors!*" That is not a coincidence. Before a pastor can be effectual in preaching, he must first pastor his people. Before he will be effective

The Art of Pastoring

in being the executive officer of the church, he must first love and encourage his people. The strength of the presumed authority of leadership is rooted in first loving and helping the people. It is called pastoring.

Chapter Two - "Shepherd the Flock!"

Pastor the flock of God which is among you.

In 1931, Walter Sorenson died an untimely and unexpected death. His second son, Henry, at the age of sixteen had the weight of supporting his mother and younger brothers thrust upon him. It was the depth of the depression. However, the coach of his high school tennis team in his senior year was able to help him locate a job as a messenger at the First National Bank of Oshkosh, Wisconsin. Henry, my father, worked full-time at the bank to help support his family.

Upon graduating from high school, he continued on at First National Bank and was promoted to the position of teller. As the years passed, he was promoted to head teller of the bank, which was the largest in the area. (Years later, the man under Dad in seniority would go on to become the president of the bank.)

One day when Dad was twenty years old, his younger brother, Austin, came home excited about how he had been recently saved. (Grandma Sorenson was a godly woman who saw to it her children attended the local American Baptist Convention church.) Austin had gotten saved not because of that liberal church, but in spite of it. He had attended a Bible class at Waupaca, Wisconsin, and invited Dad to attend the class held at the home of a retired railroad man. Austin continued to witness to Dad. One night, Dad lay awake mulling over what his younger brother had told him. There, on his bed, he opened his heart and trusted Christ as personal Savior. He, like his brother, was gloriously born again.

As a young Christian, he became active in the Temple Baptist Church of Oshkosh, Wisconsin. Dr. John R. Siemens was the dynamic pastor of the church and made a powerful impression upon Dad. He soon was elected as a deacon in the church. As time passed, he began to sense God's call upon him to preach. Not too far from Oshkosh was the small farming community of Omro, Wisconsin. A Baptist church was there but was on the verge of closing its doors. They asked Dad to come and be a pulpit-supply pastor. After driving over to Omro each weekend in his '32 Chevy for some time, the church called him as their pastor. He had no formal schooling. All he had was a love for the Lord, a love for the people, and a strong desire to serve Him. His two role models were Dr. Siemens and his soon to be father-in-law, Dr. O. P. Lovik.

Meanwhile, he had asked Viola Lovik to be his bride. They were married in the spring of 1941. (Mother's father, Dr. O. P. Lovik, was an old-fashioned, Norwegian, Baptist pastor. At the time, he was the pastor of the First Baptist Church of Winneconne, Wisconsin.) Shortly after their marriage, his wife was diagnosed with tuberculosis. It was still the day when this dreaded disease was often fatal, and indeed she lost several members of her family to TB. She spent the next eighteen months in a sanitorium recovering from the tuberculosis. During that time, God dealt with her heart, and she too submitted to the call of the ministry.

Shortly thereafter, Dad resigned his position at the bank, resigned his church, and enrolled at the Northwestern College and Seminary in Minneapolis under the leadership of the late W. B. Riley. My father often would go out on weekends and preach in

Owatonna, Minnesota. One day, Dr. Riley called him into his office and said, "Henry, First Baptist Church in Stillwater, Minnesota needs a pastor. Would you be interested?" Dad was. The necessary contact was made with the pulpit committee, and in 1944, while still a student at Northwestern, Dad became the pastor of that church. It was in June of 1946, this author was born in Stillwater, Minnesota.

My father spent eight happy years in that church. Much later in life he would confide to me it was such a happy ministry, he should never have left it. In 1953, he accepted the call to the First Baptist Church of St. Cloud, Minnesota, where he served for five years. Then in the spring of 1958, he became the pastor of the Faith Baptist Church of Pekin, Illinois, where he served for the next 31½ years. During that time, the church grew to over one thousand in a town of 30,000. He retired from the full-time ministry in 1989 and in 1990 came to Duluth, Minnesota to become a part-time assistant pastor with me, his son. It was there the Lord took him home to glory in March of 1996.

The Essence of Shepherding

In I Peter 3:1-4, the apostle wrote, *"The elders which are among you I exhort, who am also an elder, and a witness of the sufferings of Christ, and also a partaker of the glory that shall be revealed: Feed the flock of God which is among you, taking the oversight thereof, not by constraint, but willingly; not for filthy lucre, but of a ready mind; Neither as being lords over God's heritage, but ensamples to the flock. And when the chief Shepherd shall appear, ye shall receive a crown of glory that fadeth not away."*

The greater thought of I Peter 3:1-4 deals with being a pastor to the flock. I suspect this passage is not well understood by Christians in general and even preachers in particular. As a seminary-trained pastor, I did not totally understand its significance until I had been in the ministry for many years. Let us spend a little time and make running commentary upon it. Peter begins by exhorting the *elders* in the churches of Pontus, Galatia, Cappadocia, Asia, and Bithynia. He notes in verse 1 how he also was an *elder*. We soon will look in more detail at the significance of this word. However, suffice it to say at this point, the word *elder* in this context is another name for the more common term "pastor." Though the terms do have nuances of distinction, for all practical purposes, an elder in the early church was the same individual who we today would call the pastor.

In verse 2, Peter issued an imperative to the elders (pastors) he had exhorted in verse 1. The Authorized Version says, *"Feed the flock of God which is among you."* It is set forth as a command. The context clearly is of the local church and its leadership. In my view, the imperative to feed the flock is more commonly misunderstood than properly understood. Because of the way it is translated in the King James Version, the assumption is commonly made how Peter is admonishing elders in the early church (and by extension, church leadership today) to provide spiritual nourishment for the church. This is commonly understood to mean a pastor presenting well-prepared sermons and messages for the church. In so delivering messages with good biblical content, the common presumption is that a preacher is fulfilling this biblical injunction.

Though it might sound heretical, that is *not* what this passage is driving at. To be sure, a pastor ought to "preach the Word" and be a teacher thereof. The cumulative evidence of the New Testament toward that end is great. However, in this case, that is *not* what Peter had in mind. (In a later chapter we will deal at length with the responsibility of a pastor to teach and preach God's Word.)

The word translated "feed" literally means to shepherd. The confusion to a considerable degree lies in the word which is translated "feed." The word Peter used is "poimaino." It is the verbal form of the noun "poimen." As you will recall, a "poimen" was a shepherd. In its noun form, it is translated as "shepherd" 17 out of the 18 times it appears in the New Testament. The other time it is translated as "pastor" in Ephesians 4:11. The verbal form, "poimaino," simply means "to shepherd." It also is translated a number of times as "to rule," as well as several times, "to feed." It is used 11 times in the New Testament. However, the most basic sense of the word simply is "to shepherd." Shepherding in part does include seeing to it the sheep are fed. But the feeding of the sheep is secondary to the greater and more complex idea of shepherding a flock.

The emphasis is not food for the sheep, but their care. In coming to understand this principle, I Peter 5:2-3 takes on an entirely different light. The emphasis in not upon *food* for the sheep. Rather, it is upon *care* for the sheep. To shepherd is to provide care both for individual sheep as well as oversight of the greater flock. It is interesting to note at this point how Jesus used this same word in a similar context. In John 21:16, He commanded Peter to feed His sheep. He used the identical word as Peter did in I Peter 5:2. It could be translated as "Pastor my sheep," or "Shepherd my sheep." (Actually in John 21:15 and 17, the words "feed" are translated from the Greek word "bosko" which is not ambiguous. It means "to feed" in regard to a herd or a flock.) In writing to the elders in I Peter 5, Peter was in fact reiterating exactly what Jesus had personally commanded him just prior to His ascension. For all practical purposes, in both John 21 and I Peter 5, the respective texts could be essentially rendered "Pastor the sheep." To be sure, that involves providing spiritual nourishment for them. But it means much more. It is loving the people, encouraging the people, helping the people. It is being there when the people need someone. It is teaching the people, guiding the people, and correcting the people. It is building rapport with the people as well as providing oversight and direction for the flock collectively.[1]

The most basic sense of the word "poimaino" remains "to shepherd" or its ministerial sense "to pastor." Of the 62 places in the Authorized Version of the New Testament where a word has been translated in some way as "to feed," less than ten percent derive from the word "poimaino." It is the opinion of this author, every one of those cases could have been translated as "to shepherd" or "to pastor." The implications of this distinction, in my view are profound.

The primary idea is "shepherd the flock of God which is among you." Returning to I Peter 5, notice how Peter continues the thought in adding subordinates phrases. To shepherd the flock of God includes *"taking the oversight thereof."* This phrase actually derives from a word which is of interest. The verb "episkopeo" means "to take or have oversight." It is the verbal form of "episcopos" from whence the English word "bishop" is translated. Here, it has the sense of assuming oversight of God's flock, i.e., the local church. Whereas the concept of a shepherd bespeaks the care of the sheep individually, the word "episkopeo" refers to the oversight and leadership of the flock collectively. Hence, both the personal care and oversight of the flock are addressed in one sentence.

Peter continues to add secondary thoughts to the primary imperative of shepherding. He notes how they ought to do so *"not by constraint, but willingly; not for filthy lucre, but of a ready mind."* The idea is how a pastor ought to shepherd God's people not as a chore because it is his job. Neither ought he to be in the ministry because it is a source for income and a way to make a living. Rather, it is a ministry a pastor ought to discharge willingly and eagerly. The care of God's people is at stake.

A godly pastor will have right attitudes toward his people. Moreover, pastors ought not rule their people *"as being lords over God's heritage, but being ensamples to the flock."* The phrase translated *"being lords over"* has the sense of heavy handed leadership. It conveys the idea of being like a boss to God's people. (There often is a fine line between having a CEO mentality and scriptural, pastoral leadership.) The nuance of the idea is not so much of diminishing the prerogative of pastoral leadership or authority. Rather, Peter is dealing with an *attitude* of leadership which may be aloof, overbearing, or independent. What is clearly implied is how a godly pastor ought to have an attitude which presents an example of a servant's heart to his people. Implied in verse 4 is submission to the Chief Shepherd, Jesus Christ. In verse 5, the connective word *"Likewise"* links the subject of submission and humility to the preceding, giving additional insight into the example a godly pastor ought to present.

Shepherding meshes well with the idea of oversight. The conventional wisdom of feeding the flock by teaching the Word does not mesh well with the immediate succeeding thought of providing proper oversight. However, the idea of shepherding the flock and providing proper oversight goes together like hand and glove. It makes sense. It fits. Moreover, the modifying clauses of willingness and a proper attitude in leadership makes much more sense when connected to the idea of being a good shepherd. The conventional wisdom of delivering good messages somehow does not resonate as well with the same clauses of willingness and proper attitude.

In summary: it is incontrovertible, the primary thought in verses 2 and 3 is the imperative, *"Feed the flock of God."* As noted above, the basic etymology and definition of the word translated *"feed"* is to shepherd. In more ministerial terms, it simply means to pastor the people. The succeeding context makes much more sense resonating with the idea of pastoring than of message content. I would therefore submit the proper understanding of I Peter 5:2-3 is the injunction **for elders to pastor their people**. It is the thesis of this entire book.

As mentioned earlier, my father may not have been one of the great pulpiteers of his era. But he was one of the great pastors. As I graduated from being an associate pastor to a senior pastor, his basic advice to me over the years was, "Dave, pastor your people." A major key to maintaining the flock is for the preacher to be a pastor to his people. That sort of advice may not be the focal point of popular conferences. But if a preacher does not pastor his people, he will not pastor them long. Either they will leave, or circumstances will cause him to leave.

What is an Elder?

An elder is a leader. In the New Testament, three different terms are used to define the leader of the local church. The most frequently used is that of "elder" which is translated from the Greek word "presbuteros." The word "presbuteros" appears 69 times in the New Testament. However, of that number, only 18 places refer to leadership of the local church. The rest deal either with the leadership of the nation of Israel, the leadership in Jewish synagogues, or reference to older people in distinction to younger people. It is a term of presumed authority. The idea is based upon the Eastern custom of patriarchal authority of the oldest male member of a family or clan. It is related to the Eastern custom of the first-born, his prerogative, and the rank assigned thereto. The eldest male member of a family by virtue of his rank and seniority was its elder (i.e., leader).

The New Testament term "elder" draws from Old Testament usage. In Old Testament Israel, tribal leadership was deferred to the elder of the tribe. For example, note the assumed authority in such men as Isaac, Reuben, Aaron, or Pharez. By New Testament times, the Jews designated the members of the Great Sanhedrin (the ruling Council at Jerusalem) as "elders." As the synagogue system developed across the Jewish diaspora, the basic term for its leadership was that of "elder." The term as it pertains to the New Testament church clearly has its roots in the synagogue. As the church was born in the temple at Pentecost (and numerous other churches were started in synagogues), the term ascribed to its early leadership was that of elder. The earliest church initially was largely a Jewish phenomenon. Accordingly, its initial structure and leadership were patterned after the familiar synagogue.

As the church became more gentile in nature, a new term more familiar to the Greek mind began to emerge. That was "episcopos" (or "episcope"), i.e. bishop, and its verbal derivative, "episcopeo." In local church usage in the New Testament, the term "elder" (presbuteros) was never used in the sense of some governing board of directors operating over a pastor. In fact, the concept of committees and "boards" as is commonly used today is alien to New Testament polity in the early church. One will search in vain to find an even remote hint of such in the New Testament. (That is not to say the creation of committees or boards within a church are wrong. However, biblically, such groups are without authority over either the congregation or the pastoral leadership. Scripturally, the function of committees and boards are to assist and advise the church as a whole or its pastoral leadership.)

Why the term "elder" is sometimes used in the plural. The term "elder" is found frequently in plural usage. The only significance in the early church was there often were several men in leadership of a church. For example, the church at Ephesus is referred to as having "elders" (plural) in Acts 20:17. However, an understanding of the nature of the church at Ephesus and other similar places will give insight into such plural usage. In the first century, local churches as a rule did not have their own dedicated buildings. The idea of a "church building" so common today was totally alien to them. They initially met in homes or public halls. In large cities such as Ephesus, the growth of the church necessitated the utilization of homes scattered across the city to accommodate the overall body. In each of these satellite "house-churches" there usually was an elder or bishop under the overall leadership of the primary pastor. In time, these eventually became free-standing, autonomous churches. Moreover, in the earliest days of the church, paid, full-time leadership had not as yet developed.

Hence, early congregations often had several "elders" to take care of the overall ministry of the church. The fact of a plurality of elders in the early church had nothing to do with the polity of the church. Rather, it was a practical solution to problems unique to that era of church development. In modern church organization, it is quite common for a number of men to be on the church pastoral staff. One is the senior pastor, and the others have specific areas of ministry in assisting the primary pastor. To that degree, modern churches also have a plurality of elders. What clearly is implied is one overall leader who had the assistance of a number of subordinates in the ministry.

Who is a Bishop?

A bishop is the scriptural overseer of the local church. The next term of leadership is that of "bishop," translated from the Greek word "episcopos." In its various derivatives, the term appears about nine times in relation to the leadership of the local church. It is a Greek word which literally means "an overseer." It is formed from two simpler words, "epi" which is a common preposition with the sense of "over;" and "skopeo" which means "to look" or "to watch." Combining the two words into "episcopeo" or its nominative derivative, "episcopos," the idea of "watching over" or "overseeing" develops. That is the precise meaning of the English word "bishop."

As the church became more gentile in nature as the first century progressed, this term began to supersede the earlier term "elder." Both terms are used interchangeably in several places in the New Testament regarding the same individual. In all such cases, the leader of the churches was he who is commonly referred to as the "pastor" today. In Acts 20:17-35, Luke records Paul's farewell message to the summoned "elders" of the Ephesian church (20:17). However, in verse 28, Paul admonished these "elders" to *"take heed therefore unto yourselves, and to all the **flock** over the which the Holy Ghost hath made you **overseers**, to **feed** the church of God, which he hath purchased with his own blood."* In one verse, Paul admonished the elders of the Ephesian church to take heed to the church which the Holy Ghost had made them "*overseers.*" The word translated as "overseer" is "episcopos." Paul notes how the Holy Ghost had made these elders overseers or bishops of the church. Interestingly, this is the only place in the Authorized Version where the word "episcopos" is translated as "overseer." It certainly is an accurate translation. However, in every other instance, the word "episcopos" is translated as "bishop." Without a question, Paul used both terms interchangeably. Those who were elders in the church were also bishops. (It might be noted, to this degree there was a plurality of bishops here as well.)

To digress momentarily, it is of interest that Paul, in addressing the elders of the Ephesian church, noted how God had made them overseers (bishops) over the church. He further noted how God had called them "*to feed the church of God, which he hath purchased with his own blood.*" The word translated "*feed*" once again is "*poimaino*" which literally means "to shepherd." (Recall how the nominative root is "poimen" which is translated as "shepherd" or "pastor.") In essence, Paul exhorted the elders of the Ephesian church *to pastor* their people. Though the church collectively indeed has been purchased by the blood of Jesus Christ, it is the people individually who have been redeemed and cleansed by His blood. Hence, he urged these elder/overseers *to pastor* their people.

In the New Testament, the terms "elder," "bishop," and "pastor" are used interchangeably. This is a unique passage in the New Testament. Not only are the terms "elder" and "overseer" (bishop) used interchangeably, they both are directly related to the function of pastoring God's people. Thus, the three basic terms of local church leadership are found in one direct context.

In Titus 1:5-9, Paul wrote to Titus concerning the installation of "elders" (presbuteros) in every church on the island of Crete. In verse 6 and following, he set forth basic qualifications for this office. However, in verse 7 referring to the office of elder, Paul used the word "bishop" (episcopos) to refer to the same individual. The terms are used interchangeably. An elder and a bishop in a local church are one and the same person!

Of course, as has been noted at length earlier, Peter makes the case in I Peter 5:1-3 how the elders of the church are to pastor (or shepherd) it. In taking the sum total of New Testament local church usage of these three terms (elder, bishop, and pastor), it is evident they all refer to the same individual in a given church. To be sure, there are nuances of distinction which shortly will be noted. However, it should be clear. Each of these terms refers to the one who is the God-called, God-ordained leader of a local church.

What is the Pastor?

A pastor is a shepherd. The final term used in the New Testament for local church leadership is, of course, "pastor" which as noted above is translated from the Greek word "poimen." The word "poimen" appears nine times in the New Testament in a spiritual sense. Without question, its primary sense is of "shepherd." It is the word used in John 10 when Jesus discussed the Good Shepherd and His sheep. It also is the word used in referring to the Chief Shepherd in I Peter 5:4 and the Great Shepherd in Hebrews 13:20. It is translated only once as "pastor" in Ephesians 4:11. However, it certainly has the sense of shepherding there as well.[2]

What is the Difference?

The pastor. Though each of these terms refer to the same individual, each has a nuance of distinction. Inherent in the term "pastor" (or shepherd) is the idea of personal care and concern. It is a term of individual tenderness, love, and consideration. It alludes to oversight of individuals. It is this term upon which we shall seek to expand in the coming chapters.

The bishop. Inherent in the term "bishop" is the idea of oversight, both spiritual and administrative. The bishop of the church is the one God has ordained to oversee the *entire* ministry of the church. I once knew a church where the idea was articulated and advanced how the deacons were to oversee the people, the trustees were to oversee the finances, the school board was to oversee the Christian school, and the pastor was merely the hired preacher. Sadly, many a denominational church has such attitudes. However, such an idea is wrong from top to bottom. God has ordained the *bishop* to oversee every part of the church from the spiritual to the financial. That is not to say he ought not utilize duly elected officers to assist, particularly in financial matters. He should. However, in the New Testament, the only individual granted the ultimate prerogative of local church oversight is the bishop (i.e. the pastor). Of course, oversight includes much more than fiscal matters. It is the oversight of the entire ministry of the church, particularly the spiritual. At no place in the New Testament is this responsibility delegated to any board or committee, whatever its name might be. The bishop is the administrator and overseer of the local church!

The elder. The term "elder" has the historic sense of implied authority and leadership. That is not to say the "elder" (i.e. pastor) has no restraint. It does not mean he can do anything he wishes. It certainly does not mean he is dictator or king of the church. It simply implies the "elder" is the one who, by his position, holds the influence of leadership. He is the person in the vanguard who will lead the ministry. A wise "elder" (pastor) will always seek the counsel and advice of his people. The men whom God has given to serve as deacons are an invaluable source of counsel and wisdom. Other people and leaders in the church can be a constant source of feedback to enable the "elder" (i.e. pastor) to sense the pulse of the church.

The parallel to a husband and wife. A pastor and his deacons might be likened to the relationship a husband and wife may have. The Bible clearly gives leadership prerogative to the husband. But woe be to a husband who ignores his wife's counsel. When push comes to shove, he may have the ultimate prerogative to make a final decision. However, a wise husband will seek the counsel and advice of his wife. Likewise, ought an "elder" (i.e. pastor) seek the same from his deacons and other people in the church. Wise will be the pastor who so respects the input from his people. To ignore their insight and comment is inviting trouble, fast. (It should be noted in using the term "influence of leadership" that a pastor's primary authority is by influence. In most churches, the congregation holds the authority to dismiss their pastor. Hence, they are the final authority. A pastor's authority is limited to leading people through their confidence in his integrity, love, dedication, knowledge, wisdom, and influence which he exerts.)

And so as the leader of the local church wears the hat of pastor, he loves, encourages, and helps the people. As he wears the hat of bishop, he oversees and administers the overall ministry of the church. As elder, he sways the influence of leadership in leading the church.

The Pastoral Triad

A major portion of a pastor's ministry is that of preaching. In a coming chapter, we will delve into that in some detail. In a sentence, a pastor's pulpit ministry will be a significant aspect of his overall success. Yet from a practical perspective, the pastoral ministry is a triad. We might liken it to the three legs of a tripod. If one of those legs are weak or wobbly, the overall ministry of a pastor will be in trouble. I have been around the ministry for fifty years either in growing up in the parsonage or in spending the rest of my life in the pastoral ministry. As noted earlier, my father spent over fifty years in a pastoral ministry. His father-in-law, my grandfather, spent an additional fifty years in a pastoral ministry before that. Drawing from that perspective, I believe the three crucial elements of a pastoral ministry involve the following:

1. **Preaching** (i.e. the ministry of the Word and all that is involved therewith);
2. **Program management** (i.e. church administration of total church ministries);
3. **Pastoring the people** (loving, encouraging, helping, and meeting their needs).

Let us diagram this paradigm accordingly.

The Pastoral Ministry

- **Preaching** (The ministry of the Word and all involved therewith)
- **Program Management** (Church administration)
- **Pastoring the People** (Loving, encouraging and meeting their needs)

If any one of these three areas is weak or insufficient, a pastor will be in trouble. However, it is the view of this author how *many* modern pastors are weak in the matter of *pastoring* their people.

Though one might be an excellent preacher both in content and delivery, if he does not pastor his people, he will be in for a rough ride. He may be skilled in administrative and management skills. Yet, if he does not pastor his people, all of his administrative prowess may be overlooked.

Interestingly, it has been the observation of this author how men who are not the best preachers in the world but pastor their people will generally have successful ministries. Similarly, some men are not particularly skilled in the administration of their church. Yet because they pastor their people, the church overlooks or puts up with their administrative shortcomings. Though the matter of pastoring one's people is not the be-all and end-all of the ministry, it comes close. It is so simple. It is so crucial. It is profound! Yet, in the view of this author, it is frequently overlooked, particularly by young pastors.

Pastoring and Fulfilling the Great Commission

Jesus Christ told his disciples, "*I will build my church; and the gates of hell shall not prevail against it,*" (Matthew 16:18). The local church of the New Testament is the *only* body Jesus Christ has placed upon this earth since His ascension back to glory. It is the "*ground and pillar of the truth,*" (I Timothy 3:15). Or, put another way, the local church is the foundation and support of the truth.

The analogy of the church to a lighthouse. The idea of a lighthouse is a good illustration of the church. On the north shore of Lake Superior is a renowned lighthouse known as Split Rock Lighthouse. It is situated above the rocky waters of the great inland sea upon a massive rock outcropping rising vertically more than one hundred sixty feet out of the water. The lighthouse is literally built upon a rock. That rock forms the foundation of the structure which supports the third-order, Frêsnel lens which casts a beam across the great lake that can be seen up to sixty miles. What a clear illustration of the church! It is founded upon the rock of Jesus Christ and is the spiritual structure our Lord ordained to cast the light of the gospel across the troubled waters of the world. Split Rock Lighthouse was built early in the twentieth century to warn passing ships of the dangerous coastal waters of western Lake Superior. The church in part has been established to warn the lost of the danger of hell ahead.

Fifty miles to the southwest of the Split Rock light is the entry to the Duluth, Minnesota, harbor. At one time, it was the busiest port in America, shipping greater tonnage than New York or other eastern ports. Ships from all over the world to this day come and go through the harbor entrance. Situated at each side of the harbor mouth are smaller lighthouses - the proverbial "lower lights" of P.P. Bliss. Though modern ships are equipped with all manner of electronic navigational aids ranging from radar and LORAN to GPS, nevertheless the low-tech, venerable lighthouses at the harbor's mouth prove a welcome aid to mariners on dark, stormy nights. In contrast to the Split Rock light which warned of danger, these lower lights point to safety. In years past, more than one ship has been wrecked within sight of the harbor during a stormy night because the captain missed the harbor entrance. And so the church points men to the safety in heaven's haven of rest.

Because the local church of the New Testament, the foundation and support of the truth, is the exclusive body Jesus Christ has placed on this earth in this age, its leadership is crucial. A wise and famous preacher is renowned for his pithy axiom,"Everything thing rises and falls upon leadership." Though the church of Jesus Christ as an overall institution will never fail, local churches have failed. Often that failure in some way is related to its leadership. Other churches not only exist and survive, but grow great and influential. Again, their success is usually related to its leadership. Therefore, it should be evident, the office of pastor is crucial. He is the God-called, God-ordained leader of the exclusive body Jesus Christ left in His absence. Whether he wears the hat of shepherd, bishop or elder, his leadership is crucial. The well-being of the church the

The Art of Pastoring

Chief Shepherd has entrusted to him is at stake. All three of the basic functions of church leadership - preaching, program management, and pastoring of his people are vital for the ministry to go forward.

The correlation between effective pastoring and fulfillment of the Great Commission. The Great Commission given by our Lord prior to His ascension is the standing orders of the church. Jesus commanded His disciples *to disciple*. Matthew 28:19-20 is one of the several places the Great Commission is found. There He said, *"Go ye therefore, and teach all nations, baptizing them in the name of the Father, and of the Son, and of the Holy Ghost: Teaching them to observe all things whatsoever I have commanded you: and, lo, I am with you alway, even unto the end of the world. Amen."* Though the imperative would seem to be "go" and "teach," it literally is "disciple." The word translated "teach" in verse 19 is the Greek word "matheteuo." The sense is to disciple. It is presented in the imperative mode. The verse could literally be rendered, "Having gone therefore, **disciple** all peoples." It is followed by the adverbial phrases of *baptizing* and *teaching* etc. The basic thrust, however, was for the disciples (and by extension, us, today) to disciple people. It is the heart and basic imperative of the Great Commission.

The local church is the institution to which Jesus Christ gave the Great Commission. It is our standing orders. Therefore, we are under orders of our Commander-in-Chief to disciple others. If the pastor is the leader of the local church (and he is), it then follows, he has a mandate of Jesus Christ to fulfill the Great Commission. Discipling people begins by leading them to Christ. One cannot be discipled until he has been born again. The process continues as he follows the Lord in the water of baptism. However, the long term process of discipleship further continues as people are taught to observe all things whatsoever He has commanded us. The primary agent in the discipleship process is the pastor of the local church. He must set the tone of winning people to Christ. He of necessity will be the chief preacher and teacher of God's Word. He, more than anyone else, is the one who will keep the church on an even keel administratively. And he is *the one* who must pastor the people. If he does not, not much long term discipleship will take place.

People come under a pastor's ministry from several sources. Some have been won to Christ and are growing young Christians. Some have joined the church having come from elsewhere. Others have more or less grown up in the church. But it is the pastor's job to help each of these to be discipled. I would submit, if the pastor does not pastor his people, the process of fulfilling the Great Commission will be thwarted. The ministry will not go forward.

The key is for the pastor to pastor his people. Here is why. A church will tolerate average preaching. Though a pastor may not be the greatest of pulpiteers, if he is preaching the Word in sincerity, the people know they are hearing the Word of God. Guest preachers may do a better job of it. The people know their pastor is sincere and doing his best. Likewise, churches to a degree will tolerate somewhat disorderly administration if they sense their pastor has a heart for the ministry. That is not to justify sloppiness. People will put up with it if they know their pastor loves them. However, when a preacher does not pastor his people, there eventually will be a division between him and them. As that gap becomes a chasm, the work will not go forward. People will not respond well to exhortation to be doing as they ought. The soul-winning ministries of the church will not be as they ought. People in the church seem to stop growing. Though there may not be an eruption, things are not altogether right. The Great Commission is not effectively being fulfilled in the church because there is a distance between the people and their pastor.

It is like a football team where the coach and the players are not close. The coach may be very astute in the technical aspects of the game. He may know how to organize and run a team. But if he does not get close to his players, they will never perform as they would if the coach had a close relationship with them. And so it is in the church. Pastoring people by the preacher is crucial. It is crucial not

The Art of Pastoring

only for the success but the tenure of the pastor, but also for the fulfillment of the standing orders given by Jesus Christ, Himself. In the coming chapters, we will begin to look in some detail at what it means to pastor the people.

Chapter Three - Love the People!

"Though I speak with the tongues of men and of angels"

To pastor one's people is to love them. In establishing the premise that a preacher must pastor his people, the question of necessity arises - how? What does it mean to pastor people? How is it accomplished? Inasmuch as the Scripture has established this mandate, the Scripture therefore no doubt holds the answer as to how. If there is a principle in pastoring people, the profundity of which is exceeded only by its simplicity, it is the principle of love. To pastor one's people is to love them.

In my generation, there has arisen a trend to prepare those going into the ministry with the view of training professionals. I can't think of a more damaging philosophy. The ministerial landscape is littered with men who have burned out and given up in the ministry because of their professional outlook. Being a pastor is not a profession. It is a calling. It is a ministry. It is being a servant. It is loving people. Lawyers are professionals. Psychiatrists are professionals. University professors are professionals. Being a biblical pastor is not. And the pastor who has a professional mentality in the ministry is going to have a hard row to hoe. One major distinction between a professional and a biblical pastor is that a godly pastor will love his people. (Did you ever hear of a lawyer loving his client, especially when the bill is past due?)

The lesson in I Corinthians. The Apostle Paul in writing to the Corinthian church tackled a problem head on. The young church at Corinth had a distorted idea concerning the interim gifts of the Holy Spirit. (In the absence of a completed New Testament, the Holy Spirit bestowed upon the early churches special, temporary spiritual gifts to help, guide, and authenticate the church. One gift in particular was a sign of warning to unrepentant Israel - the gift of tongues.) Carnality and spiritual immaturity had caused some in the church to view their particular gift as more important than the gift to others. (Because tongues was such a vocal and noticeable gift, compared to, for example, wisdom or faith, those possessing this gift thought themselves more spiritual.) The fundamental problem was spiritual pride, which was divisive. Paul addressed this problem in I Corinthians 12-14. After seeking to put the various gifts into perspective in Chapter 12, he sets forth the ultimate solution in Chapter 13. Instead of fighting over who has the most important gift, Paul said, in effect, you ought to love each other.

The Greatest of these is Love

The love of a pastor to his people will cover a multitude of deficiencies. The problem in Bible-believing churches today is not about true spiritual gifts (though charismatic confusion certainly has caused problems over the past generation). However, many a pastor and his ministry could be greatly helped by following the injunction set forth by Paul in I Corinthians 13. A professional minister will never have the support in the ministry as a pastor who loves his people. A congregation will overlook a multitude of shortcomings in a pastor who they know loves them. Accordingly, the love of a pastor for his people will cover a multitude of deficiencies.

Love the People!

Though Paul was not addressing pastoral problems as such in I Corinthians 13, I believe there is no injustice in making application of this passage to the pastoral ministry. Without question, the context is of the local church. For the purposes of this chapter, I will apply the text to a pastor loving his people. Let us view it in that light.

"Though I speak with the tongues of men and of angels, and have not charity, I am become as sounding brass, or a tinkling cymbal. And though I have the gift of prophecy, and understand all mysteries, and all knowledge: and though I have all faith, so that I could remove mountains, and have not charity, I am nothing. And though I bestow all my goods to feed the poor, and though I give my body to be burned, and have not charity, it profiteth me nothing," (I Corinthians 13:1-3).

The missing ingredient was true spiritual love. The apostle spoke of being able to preach like an angel. He spoke of having the spiritual gifts of prophecy and knowledge so that he had complete understanding of biblical truth. Yet if he did not love his people, he was somewhere between sounding brass or less. "Sounding brass and tinkling cymbals" is an interesting metaphor. Imagine in your mind the jangling sound of oriental street music. Merchants in Eastern bazaars hired such musicians to present a carnival-like atmosphere to attract customers. Tinny trumpets accented with small, high-pitched, percussive cymbals established the "sound" of a bazaar. But it was far from soothing. It had the ambiance of hucksters seeking to con the gullible. It was a jangling sound. And it came to be idiomatic of insincerity and crass commercialism.

With that metaphor in mind, Paul spoke of being able to preach with angelic eloquence and encyclopedic knowledge. Yet he said, if he had not charity he had little more credibility than a merchant in an oriental bazaar. (Of course, we assume the reader understands how the word "charity" is translated from "agapê" and is the quintessential Greek word for "love." In each case where the Authorized Version presents the word "charity," it properly may be substituted with the word "love.")

Continuing, he noted how even if he had the gift of knowledge plus the gift of faith to the degree he could move mountains, yet if he did not love his people, he was nothing. Even if he made a great example of altruism and personal sacrifice, if he did not love his people, he was nothing. (Incidentally, so often love as a concept is defined in impersonal terms. However, love by its very nature is a relationship between *persons*. In this context, we are applying it to the relationship of a pastor to his people.)

If there is a simple key to pastoring one's people, it is to love them. If one thing could be said of my father's ministry, he loved his people. And for the most part, they loved him. It was the tie that bound.

An illustration of the opposite. In contrast, I think of a situation I was privy to some years ago. I will call him Pastor Atkins. He was an erudite man with a strong intellect. His preaching could be, for many, spell binding. Over the years, he had built the church from relative obscurity to be one of the leading churches in that region. It became relatively large and influential. Pastor Atkins' ministry had been built in part because of his eloquent exposition of the Scripture. He also was a skilled administrator in guiding the affairs of the church.

One day, as a young preacher, I sat in a meeting along with other preachers. As the conversation developed, Pastor Atkins began to speak of a family in his church who were a little out-of-sorts over some matter. It had nothing to do with doctrine, ethics, or serious principle. It seemed to be more a personality conflict. Pastor Atkins in the course of the conversation commented rather routinely how he was going "to put the hammer" on those people. I was not exactly sure what he meant, but it was quite evident by his tone, he did not intend to deal kindly with them. Because of his longevity and internal political strength, he could get away with "putting the hammer" on some of his people. In knowing him otherwise, I had reason to believe this was how he handled other problem people. Though he was in many ways a spiritual leader, one other thing sadly could be said about his ministry. His fame was not based upon a reputation for loving his people.

It was not long thereafter a major uprising erupted in that church. To make a long story short, a bitter, deep split took place. The church was seriously wounded. Pastor Atkins survived the battle, but the church never regained the strength or attendance it once had. In being privy to some of the details of that ministry, I would submit how if this preacher had loved even difficult people instead of from time to time "putting the hammer" on them, major damage to his ministry might have been prevented. A greater degree of love for his people may have prevented the uprising and split which eventually erupted. Love on the part of a pastor for his people will not only mitigate problems, it also will build a bond and strength which will preclude problems.

Love is Commanded!

The imperative of agapê love in the New Testament. The word "agapê" usually translated as "love" and its verb form "agapáo" together appear 258 times in the New Testament. It appears as an imperative numerous times. During the last hours of our Lord's life between the last supper and Gethsemane, Jesus commanded His disciples *on three separate occasions* to love one another. While seated around the table of the last supper, Jesus told them, *"A new commandment I give unto you, That ye love one another; as I have loved you, that ye also love one another,"* (John 13:34). Then, after having left the upper room and walking toward Gethsemane, Jesus said again, *"This is my commandment, That ye love one another, as I have loved you,"* (John 15:12). Shortly thereafter, He reiterated Himself again, *"These things I command you, that ye love one* *another."* If Jesus repeated the same commandment three times in the last three hours of His ministry, it would seem important.

Years later, John, by inspiration of the Holy Spirit, would repeat what he heard Jesus say that fateful night. In I John 3:23, he wrote *"And this is his commandment, That we should believe on the name of his Son Jesus Christ, and love one another, as he gave us commandment."* He further wrote, *"Beloved, if God so loved us, we ought also to love one another,"* (I John 4:11).

The Apostle Paul writing to the Ephesian church noted how he prayed regularly they might be *"rooted and grounded in love."* He then issued the imperative to *"walk in love"* (Ephesians 5:2). The author of Hebrews wrote, *"Let us consider one another to provoke unto love,"* (Hebrews 10:24). In Galatians 5:13, the apostle wrote, *"by love serve one another."*

The definition of agape. The word "agapê" (and its verbal derivative, "agapao") both may be defined as "a giving of one's self for another." Agape-love by its very nature is selfless and others-oriented. In giving of one's self, it is sacrificial. It can manifest itself across a spectrum ranging from giving to others financially, to giving of one's time, to giving of one's help, to giving of one's concern, to giving of one's very heart. It especially means a giving of kindness. The ultimate level is giving of one's life for another. This principle is richly illustrated in the Scripture. The classic example is John 3:16 wherein we read how God loved the world to such a degree *"He gave his only begotten Son."* Paul noted how Jesus loved him to such an extent, He *"gave himself for me,"* (Galatians 2:20). In Ephesian 5:2, the apostle wrote how *"Christ also hath loved us, and hath given himself for us."* In II Corinthians 12:15, Paul wrote how he was willing to *"very gladly spend and be spent for you"* because he loved the Corinthian church. The Apostle John noted how the love of God was manifested *"because that God sent his only begotten son into the world,"* (I John 4:9-10).   **Of all people, a pastor ought to love his congregation**. In each case, agape-love is illustrated by a selfless giving of one's self on behalf of the one loved. In the case of God the Father, He gave His most priceless possession, His only begotten Son, on our behalf. In the case of Jesus, He gave His very self on our behalf. In the case of Paul, he was willing to give of himself on behalf of the people to which he ministered.

Beloved, if God so loved us, we therefore ought also to love one another. And hereby perceive we the love of God, because He laid down His life for us: and we ought to lay down our lives for the brethren. I would suggest the injunction to lay down our lives for the brethren is not primarily intended to mean a sacrificing of our lives physically. Rather, it likely refers to giving ourselves for others on their behalf. If the rank and file in the pew are so enjoined to love one another, it follows that their leader in the pulpit ought to love them even more. Agape-love is a giving of ourselves to the extent we lose our lives for others. For a pastor, that means the people of his church.

If God's people in general are commanded to love one another, does not that certainly include those who are their pastors? And if anyone ought to set an example of love and lead by example in this regard, ought it not be one's pastor? If we could emulate the example of the Chief Shepherd in how He has so loved us, ought not we as pastors so love our people as His under-shepherds?

In the twentieth century, liberal, apostate Christianity has emphasized love and ignored holiness with its implications. In reacting to that, fundamentalists have often emphasized holiness and ignored love, taking it for granted. The truth is, both holiness and love need to be emphasized and practiced. In pastoring people, the principle of love is of utmost importance. It ought to be in the center of a pastor's heart for his people. It should temper and influence everything else he does in his church and particularly his regard for his people.

Another story how a lack of love hurt a pastor's ministry. I am mindful of a pastor in another state. He was a good man. He was sound in doctrine. He was a good preacher. He upheld high standards. He was above reproach in his personal ethics and integrity.

The Art of Pastoring

However, he had gotten into a circle of preachers which prided themselves on being "hard-nosed." His high standards were admirable. However, as people in his church did not live up to his high standards, he was not patient with them. He dealt in a "hard-nosed" fashion with those who did not achieve the degree of spiritual maturity he expected. He preached sharp messages on areas where people were slack. As the occasion would arise, he was quite direct and pointed in personal conversation with them in noting their lack of compliance to his goals for them. It seemed almost as if he was more concerned how his preacher-friends viewed his people, and by extension his ministry, than he was in their own spiritual well being. Seemingly, his first allegiance was the collective approval and standards of his peer group of pastor friends. His people were a means to that end.

Needless to say, his ministry was not smooth. People in his church who did not attain to standards he had set, little by little, left the church. It was not so much they were rebellious as much as they had been wounded in their spirit by their pastor's "hard-nosed" approach. As people left the church, a great deal of stress was placed upon the pastor. Though the outward standards of the church were strengthened, conformity thereto was more to avoid confrontation than out of conviction. There was something lacking in the spirit of the church. Moreover, as families left, a strain was been placed upon church finances, particularly the missions' budget.

I would submit, this dear brother and his church would have been better served if he had maintained high standards, *and* loved the people in so doing. It is a dangerous matter to try and compare one's ministry to another. The temptation becomes great for a pastor to seek the approval of other pastors of his peer group rather than loving his people and bringing them along at the pace they can handle. Paul in dealing with a similar problem wrote to the Corinthians, *"but they measuring themselves by themselves, and comparing themselves among themselves are not wise,"* (II Corinthians 10:12).

Agape-love tends to reciprocate itself. ("*We love him because, he first loved us.*") As a pastor will love his people, in due season, they will come to love him. As people love their pastor, they will tend to follow his leadership and the standards he seeks to establish. The cursor comes right back to a pastor loving his people.

How Paul described agapê-love. Paul noted how agape-love "*suffereth long, and is kind.*" The word translated "suffereth long" (makrothumeo) has the simple sense of being patient. Moreover, a quintessential element of agape-love is kindness. The old adage of catching more flies with honey than with vinegar remains. To be sure, the ministry is not catching flies. However, a pastor will have a far more effective ministry with his people by being kind to them, than by being sharp. If there is one thing which could be said about my father, he was kind to his people. His very demeanor bespoke kindness. The people knew it and responded to it. Though there were times when he had to lay down the law and take a stand, I cannot ever recall any time when he was not kind. Even as he would from time to time preach to deal with some problem, it always was delivered in a spirit of kindness. There was not a sharp or nasty bone in him.

Paul wrote how agape-love "*seeketh not her own.*" My father always was more concerned for his people than he was of his own ministry. He never viewed his present situation as a stepping stone to a greater ministry. Over the years, there certainly were people who made his ministry difficult. (Someone has said, the ministry would be great, if it weren't for the people. But the ministry is dealing *with* people. That's what it's all about.) The apostle wrote how agape-love "*beareth all things, believeth all things, hopeth all things, endureth all things.*" I know for a fact the heavy burden my father carried as a pastor. But because he (1) loved the Lord, (2) loved the people individually and (3) loved the church collectively, he bore those burdens. Any pastor who has been in the ministry any length of time knows there come days when the temptation to either (a) quit or (b) seek a different place can be great. Agape-love for the people individually and the church collectively enables us to endure all things. It truly will cover a multitude of problems.

To Shepherd is to Love

Shepherding is to give of oneself for the people. Jesus described himself as the Good Shepherd (John 10:11). In Hebrews 13:20, He is referred to as the *great shepherd of the sheep.* Peter referred to Him as the *chief Shepherd* (I Peter 5:2). It would be good if each human shepherd realized he is an under-shepherd. As a pastor, I have had to remind myself more than once, I am where I am because the Chief Shepherd put me there. Yet, I am brought back to the simple fact, the Chief Shepherd knows all about my situation. He is in charge. I am merely one of his under-shepherds.

Continuing, Jesus said, *"the good shepherd giveth his life for the sheep,"* (John 10:11). The Scripture clearly teaches how Jesus left for us an example, that we should follow in his steps (I Peter 2:21). Paul in writing to the Romans noted how God has purposed for us to be conformed to the image of His Son (Romans 8:29). Put in other words, it means God wishes us to be like Jesus. If He is the chief Shepherd and I an under-shepherd, it therefore follows, I am under an injunction to pattern my ministry after His. Now notice how Jesus said, He as the good Shepherd would give his life for the sheep. Several comments on that text therefore become imperative. Though we might seem to strain at semantics, I would suggest the text implies more than the obvious allusion to our Lord's substitutionary death upon Calvary. To be sure that is implicit. However, it is this author's view, much more is implied therein.

The word translated *"giveth"* is from the base "tithemi." It conveys the sense of "to lay down" or "to lay aside." To lay down one's life could quite accurately be rendered as "giving it" as presented in the Authorized Version. However, the conjugation of the verb is in the present tense and not the future tense. Jesus did ***not*** say, "the good shepherd *will give* His life for the sheep." Rather, the nuance of the present tense is how "the good shepherd *is giving* His life for the sheep." Moreover, that ongoing giving was already taking place as further implied by the present tense. Though, no doubt, there is inherent a prophetic element regarding Calvary, Jesus seemed to imply, He as Good Shepherd was already giving of Himself for the sheep. In so noting this shade of nuance, we have come perilously, if not synonymously, close to the definition of agape-love. Recall, how it is defined as a giving of one's self for another. What seems clearly implied is how Jesus, as Good Shepherd, loved His sheep to the extent He gave *of* Himself for them. That is, He loved them.

Giving our lives for others. Continuing, the word used by Jesus for *"life"* is the word "psyche." The primary word chosen by the Holy Spirit regarding "life" in the New Testament overwhelmingly is "zoe." Though the word "psyche" is occasionally translated as "life," it most frequently is rendered as "soul." The distinction between the two at this point is that "psyche" refers to the *overall nonphysical being*, whereas "zoe" is the *actual life* of that being. For example, in the context at hand, Jesus said in verse 10 how He was come that they might have *life*, and that they might have it more abundantly. The word translated "life" in verse 10 is "zoe." However, in verse 11, Jesus used the word "psyche" in speaking of giving his life for the sheep.

With that in view, the essence of what Jesus said in verse 11 is how He as the Good Shepherd was giving of Himself *for* His sheep. That is the essence of agape-love. In several places in the gospels, Jesus spoke of losing one's life for His sake. For example, in Luke 9:24, Jesus said, *"But whosoever will lose his life for my sake, the same shall save it."* The word used here (as well as in the other gospels at this point) is "pysche." Jesus was not speaking particularly of dying physically. Rather, He spoke of a total giving of one's life for His sake. As we love Him to the point we are willing to give our all, we lose our life in His. It is the view of this author, our Lord in

The Art of Pastoring

John 10:11 referred to giving His life for the sheep in this regard as well as the cross.

He loves His sheep to such a degree, He has given His all for us. That led ultimately to Calvary. It is highly unlikely we as under-shepherds will ever have to face that ultimate sacrifice on behalf of our congregation. But Jesus did because He loved His sheep to such an extent He gave of His very life for them. Under-shepherds today will likely never go to a cross for their sheep. However, if Jesus is an example for us, we therefore ought to love our people to the degree we are willing to utterly give of ourselves for their sakes.

Love the people more than the program. Jesus then proceeded to refer to hirelings and their attitude toward the sheep. A hireling is essentially another term for an assistant. A hired hand likely will not have the sacrificial love for the sheep the shepherd does. As Jesus noted in John 10:12-13, when trouble looms, the hireling becomes more concerned for his own hide than for the sheep. I certainly do not wish to speak unkindly of assistant pastors. I was one for some years. However, one thing I have observed in assistant pastors over the years is how their focus often is largely upon their particular *program*. A mature pastor by distinction will tend to focus on the *people*. There is, for example, a tendency among music directors to focus on the music program rather than upon the people who comprise the music ministry. The same could be said about youth pastors or any other type of ministerial assistant. The tendency is to use the people available to make their particular program shine. An inclination develops to do whatever is necessary to ensure their assigned program succeeds. The people become a means to that end. A seasoned pastor by distinction will focus upon his people and view programs in the church as a means to help them.

Jesus went on to note how the hireling *"careth not for the sheep."* This is intended as a criticism of no one, including those on church staffs. However, the point Jesus sought to make is how a good shepherd will care for his sheep. He will love them. He will sacrifice himself for their benefit.

Love the People!

Pastoral Love is Sacrificing for the People

Love means sacrifice. One thing I learned from my father was the necessity to sacrifice of myself for my people. There were frequent times during Dad's ministry when he jumped up from a meal to head for the hospital because one of his people had been taken to the emergency room. There were many a night when he was roused in the wee hours to go and help one of his people. There were times when he cut vacations short to hurry home to meet the needs of his people. There were several times over the years when he dropped whatever and took off for up to a week to be with people in the church who had been suddenly bereaved with an out-of-state funeral. A day off was something he never much observed. When the people had need, he was there. He never failed to make daily visits when his people were in the hospital. They needed someone to pray with them and love them. If he found out someone was discouraged, he was at their door to pray with them.

When businessmen in the church were teetering on the brink of foreclosure, he was always there to pray with them and seek heaven's help in their crisis. There are a number of them to this day who are in prospering businesses. Yet, they would long ago have closed their doors had it not been for crisis prayer meetings with their pastor on their knees in his study. There were times when he opened his wallet and either loaned or just gave money to people in the church in their times of financial crisis. If loving people is a giving of one's self for the other, that includes giving of our substance for them. Dad did on more than one occasion. He cared for his sheep. On one occasion, he had the grisly task of cutting down a man who had hanged himself. He had gone to encourage him. Tragically, the man had committed suicide before he got there. There were the sobering times of having to sit down with family members and inform them their loved one had died. There were the hours of sitting with his people in hospital waiting rooms praying with them and just being with them. He gave his life for his sheep.

The Art of Pastoring

How not loving one's people brought serious trouble. I am mindful of a pastor friend in another state. He had been successful in building a church. When the opportunity arose to candidate at a much larger and influential church, he jumped to the occasion. It was his chance to go "big-time." He received the call and moved to the new place. However, I honestly think the matter went to his head. The church was in a suburban area of a well-known city. The church had multiple ministries which gave it a large overall budget. It truly was a corporation in the secular sense of the word. Scores of people were employed by its ministries. Moreover, influential people in the community attended there.

However, this pastor came to view himself as the chief executive officer (CEO) of the corporation. (Legally and organizationally, indeed he was.) He tried to run the overall ministry as a businessman would run a business. He brought in his own "team" for the church staff. But in so doing, numbers of faithful, long-time members of the church were let go. Too bad. If a staff member was not up to speed, he fired him. He insisted upon an increase in his salary commensurate with what other executives in the area were earning. He always drove a late model, up-scale automobile like other executives drove. His suits were impeccable, expensive business suits. His shoes were the finest. He bought a *very* nice, new home in a trendy, up-scale part of town. Because the services of the church were broadcast, he viewed himself additionally as a local celebrity.

This Bible-believing pastor had so imbibed the chief-executive-officer mentality, he was more a full-time CEO than pastor. The delicate ministry of being a pastor to his people had faded from his view. (And it was not unnoticed by the people in the church.) If a member of the church wished to see him, no matter how long they had been in the church, they had to wade through first the receptionist, the church secretary, and finally the pastor's secretary. They whereupon found out if they did not have an appointment, the pastor might not see them.

If ordinary people in the church were in the hospital, an assistant pastor would come to visit them. However, if the sick person happened to be wealthy, the pastor himself made a point to visit them. That preferential treatment eventually leaked out into the church. It did not cause his stock to rise. The pastor was too busy to visit in the homes of his own people. When there were deaths in the church, assistant pastors were assigned to do the funeral and the pastor often did not even appear at the visitation. He had his secretary send a card of condolence on his behalf. However, once again, if the deceased was affluent or otherwise was well-connected, the pastor himself officiated the funeral. Again, such preferential treatment did not go unnoticed.

The church was accustomed to a pastor-led type of ministry in distinction to a board-run type of ministry. However, after time, deacons who should have had some knowledge of significant financial dealings knew nothing about them. When several deacons finally got up enough courage to confront this in a deacons' meeting, the pastor rudely brushed them aside. He intimidated them by demanding, "Do you question my integrity?" Though he then belatedly informed the deacons of financial decisions he had made, a crack in the ministry was beginning to open. His decisions may have been proper and for the financial good of the ministry. Nevertheless, he did not have the courtesy (or wisdom) to keep his deacons up to speed. His rude handling of those who questioned his decisions was noted by other deacons who were not otherwise upset. The pastor just bulldozed ahead, pushing questions or objections aside.

It does not take a rocket scientist to figure out this man was heading for trouble. Over a period of several years, many people left the church. Though it was a large church, numbers of the remainder noticed their thinning ranks. Things ultimately came to a head when an influential deacon in the church forced a showdown in an open business meeting. There were nasty charges and countercharges made. When it was over, many more people left the church. The pastor survived. A majority of the people sided with him. Yet, the church had been seriously wounded. The pastor was a good preacher. He was doctrinally sound. He was moral. His personal life was above reproach in-so-far as ethics, finances, and family were concerned. But he did not exercise tender care and love for his people. They were the congregation in the pew. He was the CEO in the office. His difficulties stemmed in large part from a lack of real love for his people. His CEO mentality precluded him from genuinely pastoring them. Tragically, the testimony of that church was damaged. He was sadder but wiser.

Paul Loved his People

A pastor's heart. The apostle Paul was primarily a missionary, soul winner, church planter and preacher. Nowhere in the New Testament is he ever noted as being a pastor as such. However, as he would go into a community to preach, win people to Christ, and begin to disciple them, he inevitably performed many of the functions of a pastor. As he got many churches started and maturing, he in effect was their first pastor. It usually was not long. But until a pastor could be installed, he functioned in that regard before moving on to the next place.

In later writing to the church he founded at Thessalonica, Paul bared his heart to them. In so doing, he revealed the heart of a pastor even though he was not with them a long time. Let's read his comments to them in I Thessalonians 2:7-13.

> *"But we were gentle among you, even as a nurse cherisheth her children: so being affectionately desirous of you, we were willing to have imparted unto you, not the gospel of God only, but also our own souls, because ye were dear unto us. For ye remember brethren, our labour and travail: for labouring night and day, because we would not be chargeable unto any of you, we preached unto you the gospel of God. Ye are witnesses, and God*

also, how holily and justly and unblameably we behaved ourselves among you that believe: As ye know how we exhorted and comforted and charged everyone of you, as a father doth his children, That ye would walk worthy of God, who hath called you unto his kingdom and glory. For this cause also thank we God without ceasing, because, when ye received the word of God which ye heard of us, ye received it not as the word of men, but as it is in truth, the word of God, which effectually worketh also in you that believe.

There is much which is germane to the discussion at hand. Notice how Paul and Silas (and possibly Timothy) "were gentle among you, even as a nurse cherisheth her children." The word translated "gentle" (epios) has the sense of being gentle of spirit or mild mannered. The word translated "nurse" (trophos) is not in the sense of a registered nurse as we might think today. Rather, the idea was of a nursing mother with her bond of love and kindness for her child. The great apostle, perhaps the greatest preacher and soul winner of all time, the one taken up into the third heaven seeing things not lawful for man to utter, the one who wrote more of the New Testament than any other one man, was yet gentle, kind, and loving to those he initially pastored. A great example for the modern pastor is set forth.

Continuing, Paul wrote how he was "affectionately desirous" of them. The word so translated (himeiromai) has the sense "to lovingly long for." The people "in the pew" at Thessalonica were not just numbers on the attendance board to Paul. They were dear to him. He loved them. He longed for them. Though absence indeed makes the heart grow fonder, Paul loved them even while he was at Thessalonica. Though his missionary pastorate was not long, it was characterized by love and concern for them.

He gave of himself for his people. He then notes how he was willing to impart not only the gospel, "but also our own souls, because ye were dear unto us." The word translated "imparted" (metadidomi) is a derivative of the more basic root "didomi." The latter has the sense, "to give." Paul in effect said, "We were willing to give our own souls unto you." We come perilously close once again to the basic definition of agape-love, a giving of one's self for another. In coming to Thessalonica, Paul imparted to the young church not only the gospel, but also his very soul. (Recall how Jesus spoke of the good Shepherd giving his "soul" for the sheep.) He poured out his soul for them because they were dear unto him. The word translated "dear" (agapetos) is a derivative of the root, "agape." It has sense of "beloved" or the object of one's love. Paul loved the *people* of the church at Thessalonica. It resulted in him giving of *himself* for them. It manifested itself in being gentle and kind to them.

He encouraged his people. In verse 11, he recalled how in preaching and teaching there, I "exhorted and comforted and charged every one of you, as a father doth his children." There is notable insight into the tone of his ministry. Paul noted in verse 10 how his Thessalonian converts witnessed how *"holily and justly and unblameably we behaved ourselves among you."* In other words, he reminded them how they had no cause for criticism of his ministry. In that context, he reminded them further how his ministry was threefold. Note, he *"exhorted and comforted and charged every one of you, as a father doth his children."* The three words (1) "exhorted," (2) "comforted," and (3) "charged" are of interest. The best illustration might be a father watching his son in an athletic contest. He sits in the stands and urges, cheers, and watches him go against the competition. Through it all, there is a spirit of love, parental-pride, and enthusiasm.

The word translated "exhorted" (parakaleo) has a number of nuances. However, in this context, it essentially has the sense of "urging on" or "cheering on" like a dad cheering his son on the soccer team. The word translated "comforted" (paramutheomai) conveys an even greater degree of personal interest. It essentially has the sense of "encouraging." Once again, picture a dad on the sidelines encouraging his son as he battles the competition on the field. Finally, the word translated "charged" (marteureo) is actually the word commonly translated as "to witness." Paul in effect noted how he witnessed them grow and develop. And just as a father will watch, urge, and encourage his children, Paul used the same basic idea to explain how he coached the young church at Thessalonica.

He pastored the people. What is evident was his heart for the people. He loved them. He variously was kind and gentle, willing to sacrifice of his very self for them. He cheered them on. He encouraged them. He watched them grow. His ultimate goal was *"that they would walk worthy of God,"* (verse 12). However, the point to be noted was the tone of his ministry to his people. There was a pervasive spirit of love, kindness, encouragement, and self-sacrifice. As noted earlier, though Paul was never a pastor in the formal sense of shepherding a congregation over the long haul, without a question, he had a pastor's heart in the relatively short times he ministered to people in each locale. This is the heart a pastor ought to have. It is what it means to pastor one's people. It is loving them, helping them, cheering them on, and encouraging them. A pastor who will frame his ministry around such a heart will have a warm and productive ministry in any place.

This is what Paul wrote to the Corinthians as being the *"more excellent way,"* (I Corinthians 12:31). Though the spiritual gifts noted in I Corinthians 12-14 long ago have faded away, *"now abideth faith, hope, charity, these three; but the greatest of these is charity,"* (I Corinthians 13:13). A pastor without a heart of love for his people will eventually be found to be sounding brass and a tinkling cymbal. There without fail will come trouble from the friction of personalities not lubricated with agape-love. Without a question, a pastor needs to stand for the faith, and having done all to stand. He needs to set forth hope before the people. But the virtue which will lubricate the inevitable friction arising between leadership and those led, is the anointing oil of agape-love. It will cover a multitude of shortcomings.

The Art of Pastoring

The apostle wrote how in the inter-personal relationships of which a church is built, the greatest virtue is love. It is the position of this author how the pastor must set the tone and lead by example in loving his people. Trouble awaits a pastor who fails in this crucial essential.

Chapter Four - Help the People!

"Comfort ye my people, saith your God."

Having established how a New Testament pastor ought to shepherd and love God's people, let us consider a number of practical outworkings of the matter. The thirty-fourth chapter of Ezekiel presents an Old Testament perspective of shepherding people. The prophet wrote:

> *"And the word of the LORD came unto me saying, Son of man, prophesy against the shepherds of Israel, prophesy, and say unto them, Thus saith the Lord God unto the shepherds; Woe be to the shepherds of Israel that do feed themselves! Should not the shepherds feed the flocks? Ye eat the fat, and ye clothe you with the wool, ye kill them that are fed: but ye feed not the flock. The diseased have ye not strengthened, neither have ye healed that which was sick, neither have ye bound up that which was broken neither have ye brought again that which was driven*

away, neither have ye sought that which was lost; but with force and with cruelty have ye ruled," (Ezekiel 34:1-4)

Here, the people were Old Testament Israel (specifically Judah), and the shepherds were likely the remaining leadership of the nation of Judah. Historically, Judah as an independent nation was in its final throes of destruction at the hands of the Babylonians. Two of the three incursions against Jerusalem had already been made by the Babylonians. As Ezekiel wrote from captivity within Babylon, he warned the remnant still in the land of the final impending incursion. Precisely who the "shepherds of Israel" were is not clear. During the interval from about 605 B.C. to 586 B.C., Babylon made three successive onslaughts against Judah. Three kings ruled then: Jehoiakim, Jehoiachin, and Zedekiah. The shepherds alluded to by Ezekiel may have included them and their princes. In any event, the shepherds most likely were those in positions of authority and power in the land. [3]

The simple case presented in Ezekiel 34:1-4 is God chastening the shepherds of Israel for not properly shepherding their flock. The context once again bears this out. In verse 4, the charge is made how these self-directed shepherds (i.e. leaders) essentially were not helping their flocks. To the contrary, they took advantage of them.

A scriptural pastor ought to help his people. For New Testament pastors, the problem may not be so much taking advantage of their flocks. However, a case could be made how some pastors will not go much out of their way to help their people. That is where this chapter is going. If a pastor loves his people as he ought, it follows, he will help them. As Isaiah noted in 40:1, *"Comfort ye my people, saith your God."* The old English word "comfort" essentially has the more modern sense, "encourage." Hence, for all practical purposes, God urged encouragement for His people through the prophet Isaiah. A New Testament pastor who would help his people, must of necessity be regularly encouraging them. A famous pastor has a little saying he often quotes: "Be kind

Help the People!

to everyone, because everyone is having a tough time." It certainly is true. This particular pastor made it a practice to encourage or help his people at every opportunity he could. He accordingly has had a happy, long-term ministry. In the next chapter, we will consider how a pastor ought to encourage his people from the pulpit. However, let's look at seven specific ways in which a pastor can help and encourage his people apart from the pulpit.

1. Seek out those who are discouraged, lonely, or troubled. In every church, there are people who are lonely. Some because of circumstances are discouraged. Others face prospects in life which are troubling. A godly pastor ought to either make contact with these, or make sure someone else does. As a pastor, my father made it his business to know about the people in his church. It began by visiting them. He got to know them. He took an interest in them. As a seasoned pastor, he could spot trouble on the countenance of his people. There often was that look in their eyes. He could sense when an individual or family was discouraged. He went to find out why. He took note of those who lived alone or became shut-in.

If he were here to be interviewed, I think he would concur with me some of the sweetest rewards in the ministry were in visiting elderly people to just encourage and love them. He taught me to drop in periodically on such people. They almost universally were delighted to have their pastor come and visit. Some of the dearest friends we have made in our lives were elderly people we made a point to visit from time to time. Later, when times of financial need came in the ministry, these same people were willing to give generously to God's work. (That certainly ought not be the motive for ministering to elderly. But these dear people do not forget those who minister to them in their sunset years.)

Take note of men in the church who are unemployed. There are few things more discouraging for a man than the prospect of long-term unemployment, particularly when there seems little hope. Good, godly men in this circumstance can easily become discouraged to the point of despair. Therefore, we, from time to time, have sought out those who either were unemployed or under-employed. As my father did, I visit them in their home to have prayer with them. We may go out for lunch or coffee. I always have tried to keep my ear to the ground about possible job leads. Most people are hired because of a personal contact or word of mouth. When I hear of a company looking for help, I always take note. There might be someone in the church looking for work. Even if whatever I mention does not pan out, at least, people know I have tried to help them.

Single people in the church may be lonely. At times, men in the church are going through a time of transition in their lives. They have just been discharged from the military. They just came home from college. They just were widowed. My father taught me to show them attention. They need a friend. We seek them out, have Bible studies together, or just meet for coffee. When the lonely party was a woman, we would take our wives and try and encourage her. Those little seeds of kindness and encouragement can blossom in the most unexpected ways later. But without regard to any future "payback," the fact people have a need ought to be motive enough to try and help them.

I think of one particular widow which I had the privilege to pastor some years ago. She was old enough to be my grandmother. She had been a public school teacher for years. When retirement age came, she then began to teach in our Christian school where she continued another thirteen years. Finally, in her late seventies, her general health became such she had to retire altogether. Because she had spent much time on her knees over the decades, her knees were wobbly in her advanced years. It got to the point, where it was hard for her to make it to church at all. She lived alone. Therefore, this pastor stopped *briefly* and had prayer with her every Saturday morning about ten. Several years later, she went home to be with the Lord. But in her final years, she became fiercely loyal to her young pastor and upheld him before the throne of grace countless hours.

2. **Always be available.** Having been around the gospel ministry for over fifty years, it never ceases to amaze me when I hear stories of pastors and their "professional" attitude toward the ministry. Dad took the position he was a minister. On his calling cards, he had imprinted the comment Jesus made, *"Not to be ministered unto, but to minister,"* (Matthew 20:28). The several words translated as "minister" in the New Testament all have the general sense of being a servant. Therefore, Dad always sought to make himself available to his people.

There were several times over the years when he was on vacation in another state and word came of a death back home. (He always left word where he could be reached in an emergency.) Dad promptly packed his bags and headed home to be with the people who were bereaved and performed the funeral.

At one point in his ministry, a close relative of a man in the church died in another state. The man was beside himself with grief. Dad knew it would take three or four days, but he dropped his daily routine, made sure someone would cover the midweek service, and drove with his bereaved member to the next state. He spent time with him there encouraging and helping him even hundreds of miles from home. He felt it was important to make himself available to his people when they needed him.

I think of another pastor. I will call him Pastor Solon. He was a strong Bible believer. He was quite adequate in the pulpit. Moreover, he was a good administrator of his growing church. He also had started a Christian school, and it was flourishing. Pastor Solon was very much involved in the regional and state association of which his church was a part. Because he was politically oriented, he was always willing to assume associational duties, and because his church was one of the more prosperous within the association, he rose through its ranks. He became a part of the state board of directors of the association. Because of his considerable involvement in associational affairs, he usually was gone at least one day a week for associational meetings. At least one Monday a quarter, the

The Art of Pastoring

regional association officers met. That involved traveling. Then there were monthly meetings of the state board of directors. There were also meetings for various committees and sub-committees. Furthermore, he was an officer in the state association of Christian schools which had regularly scheduled meetings. He became involved in the national association of churches with which he was affiliated.

The upshot of it all was he was gone on quasi-church business much of the time. It might be argued how all the various associational and committee meetings were extensions of the church which he pastored. However, the simple fact remained, Pastor Solon was so busy with all of the church associational affairs, he did not have much time to spend pastoring his people. As has been the case of too many pastors, the local church which he pastored became a de facto front-organization for other activities related to the church by name.

Pastor Solon had admonished his people straightly on numerous occasions how they were not to disturb the pastor on his day off. In his case, he took each Monday off when many of the associational meetings were scheduled. He justified his heavy involvement in associational affairs by noting much of it took place on his day-off. However, there nevertheless were adjunct duties pertaining to the associations which occupied his time and energy through much of the rest of each week. Moreover, he wound up taking time off otherwise just to recharge his batteries.

One day, a faithful man in his church died - on a Monday. Because Pastor Solon had made such an issue of never disturbing the pastor on his day off, and because he let it be known to the church otherwise how busy he was, the bereaved widow dared not call her pastor until the next day. Therefore, on Tuesday morning, she called the church office to notify the pastor of her husband's death. That poor widow spent that first day and night without any pastoral support. She turned to others for help. But she dared not call her own pastor. Though she observed the announced policy, the whole affair did not sit well with her or others in the church. Pastor Solon's rigid policy did not cause his long-term stock to go up with his people. Things of that nature slowly unraveled his ministry. A gap began to widen between him and his people. He ultimately left the church and went elsewhere.

One thing I learned from my father was to have a flexible day-off policy. Any potential day off for Dad was always subordinate to the needs of the church. If something needed attention on Monday (which it usually did), he tended to it. He would try and relax at other times. But his own relaxation and interests were *always* subordinated to the needs of the people. He indeed was there not to be ministered unto, but to minister.

3. Be prompt and faithful in hospital visits. Any time someone connected with the church was in the hospital, Pastor Sorenson was there to visit them. To young, aspiring preachers ambitious to build a growing church, something so mundane as hospital visits often seems to be of secondary importance. However, Dad always stressed to me how important such visits were. Being at a bedside for prayer, encouragement, and support can do more to build a bond and rapport between a pastor and families in his congregation than probably any other one thing. The stability of a pastor's tenure is built upon the cumulative support and loyalty of the families in the church. Hospital visits are a marvelous way to build such support and loyalty.

It is important to be prompt in visiting people during their hospital stays, responding as quickly as possible. The truth is, we never know the severity of the infirmity. It is dangerous to assume the problem is routine and we can visit tomorrow. Sometimes that is the case. Sometimes people never make it out of the emergency room alive. One evening while eating supper with my family, the phone rang. A man in the church was on the other end and said, "Pastor, they have taken my mother to the hospital. They don't know what's wrong with her." I gulped down the rest of my hamburger as I headed straight for the hospital. By the time I got there, she was gone. She evidently had had a heart attack. I had the poignant experience which most pastors have had of giving on-the-spot condolence and comfort to a family suddenly bereaved. Had I waited, I would never have had the opportunity to help those people in their hour of shock and bereavement. People will forget various preachers, but they will never forget a pastor who is *there* when a loved one dies. Most hospital visits are less dramatic, but they are important nevertheless.

If a member of the church winds up in a large specialty hospital many miles away, still make it a point to visit. I recall a fellow in the church who eventually was diagnosed with a form of cancer. His doctor therefore referred him to a well-known hospital in St. Louis 175 miles away. Their pastor made a number of trips there to visit the member of his church.

I have had the experience on more than one occasion to travel considerable distance to visit people of our church in a far away hospital. Such visits had a profound influence. As mentioned above, such visits help build a bond of support and loyalty between a pastor and his people. It is a golden opportunity for a pastor to strengthen his ministry with his people. I know for a fact, I have helped build loyalty, even fierce loyalty, by being there in a distant hospital when people were in a crisis.

Hospital visits are a means of accomplishing at least three spiritual objectives. First, hospital visits are obviously to encourage and comfort. This includes the patient, but just as importantly the family. I have never met anyone who enjoyed being in the hospital. As nice as modern hospitals can be, everyone wants to get out as soon as they can. Hospitalization is a time of crisis in people's lives. The crisis is usually medical in nature, but often there is the hidden crisis of the shocking medical bills they know are coming. There frequently is a family crisis. A spouse, a mother or father, a son or daughter is lying there upon a hospital bed. And the rest of the family is troubled by it all.

Therefore, a visit to the hospital bedside is *always* a time for encouragement. It always is a time for sympathy and empathy. It always is a time to show kindness. It usually is appropriate to read Scripture, perhaps some Psalm of comfort. It *always* is appropriate to pray for the patient. As most veteran pastors know, there certainly are times when all that can be done is silent prayer. There are times when just showing up is encouragement. People in intensive care units often are not up to much conversation. But just showing up and praying for them is encouragement. There are few times in life when a person appreciates hearing someone praying for them more than on a hospital bed. It is a golden opportunity for a pastor to build rapport with people.

There are numerous times of visiting people who either are not saved or are only slightly connected with the church. But kind, sympathetic bedside visits and prayer pave the way for a greater ministry to them after they are released from the hospital.

Second, hospital visits are an opportunity to edify the spiritually mature. Visiting hospitalized people of the church who are of some spiritual maturity affords an excellent opportunity to strengthen them. They already know the Lord. They know they are in His hands. It is a good time to encourage them how such events can be stepping stones to greater faith. Because of their infirmity, they have special need. It is always a blessing to help God's people to focus upon the Great Physician who can do exceedingly, abundantly above all that we ask or think. But for those who truly are saints, it can be a time of blessing in rejoicing in the Lord and how He is able to overcome their illness.

Both my father and I have had blessed experiences over the years of visiting some dear saint upon hospital beds to encourage them, and to the contrary, they encouraged us. I certainly have visited my share of whiners and complainers. However, it is a rare gem to visit dear (usually old) saints who have only been drawn closer to the Lord by their hospitalization. Such visits become a double-edged sword. The infirm are edified by the pastor. But the pastor is edified by the godly spirit of the patient. I think of one dear saint who was up in years. She loved the Lord and was not afraid to let anyone know. As age and illness took their toll, she was hospitalized. I dutifully went to visit her and have prayer with her. Yet, though she was seriously ill, her godly spirit, her focus of faith upon her Savior, and the Scripture on the tip of her tongue caused us both to have a private revival in her hospital room. I had gone to edify her. But in the process, she edified me.

Third, hospital visits are an opportunity to win souls. Over the years, Dad led many people to Christ while visiting in hospitals. In some cases, they were people who had a "shirt-tail" connection to the church - a friend or family member of someone in the church, or perhaps someone who had visited the church. If they were well enough to be confronted with the gospel, Dad did so. He led numerous people to Christ who were the roommates of someone he had gone to visit. (He always tried to have prayer with people in the other bed. They almost always appreciated it.) On other occasions, he led family members to Christ who were there to visit. Extended times in a surgical waiting room became a fertile place for him to present the gospel. There were numbers of people in the church whom he had won to Christ visiting them in the hospital.

4. Be there when there is a death! It has been my observation how some pastors view a death in the church merely as the duty (and honorarium) of performing a funeral. And even then, the funerals are perfunctory. I have attended funerals conducted by liberal clergy which were almost nauseating. Even unsaved people were put off by the perfunctory, cold, and aloof manner of the "reverend" officiating.

When someone in the church died, it was my father's policy to get over to visit the family *as soon as possible* upon hearing of the death. He was there, if possible, before funeral arrangements were made. There is no time in life when people are more devastated and grief-stricken than the sudden death of a close family member. There is no time when people need a godly pastor more than at this time. He taught me to drop whatever I was doing and get over to be with

Help the People!

the bereaved, ASAP. People in such situations may need a little privacy, but they also need their pastor. Woe be the pastor who ignores such situations.

There have been numerous times over the years when I have rushed to sit and pray with a newly bereaved member of our church. Apart from prayer and perhaps a brief Scripture reading, there often is little else a pastor can do, but just being there is important. As word begins to get out, family and friends will start to arrive. Often in the initial hour or two after a death, the survivor is all alone. A pastor who can get there will have a tremendous opportunity to minister. The family may be in shock. They may be numb. But just the fact their pastor is there to help is a blessing. Phone calls can be fielded or made. Suggestions of where to turn for a funeral home at times can be most helpful. Just being of emotional and spiritual support until other family can arrive can be most appropriate.

The funeral can be another golden opportunity to console and help the family. It is not difficult to preach the funeral of a godly saint who has slipped into heaven's gate. It is encouraging for the family to be reminded how their loved one is now with the Lord. Dad taught me to always make the funeral a time for encouragement and strength for the bereaved. It once again was a golden opportunity to minister to them. The deceased already was wherever he or she was going to be. Make the funeral a benefit for those who are alive and can hear. That includes preaching the gospel, but it also definitely means encouraging the family.

Another thing my father taught me (which I think not many pastors do) was to follow up on the bereaved after the funeral. Funerals follow a predictable pattern. There is usually the shock of the death followed by the chaos of funeral arrangements and the tedious details of notifications. Then comes the funeral itself which ranges from impromptu family reunions to large fellowships at the church afterwards. Eventually, all the family and friends drift away. Little by little, the details of tying up loose ends are taken care of. Then a week or two later, the bereaved is alone. *Then* the loneliness

The Art of Pastoring

and the reality of the loss begins to sink in. And it is *then* when the bereaved need help as much, if not more, than during the days on each side of the funeral. A wise pastor will make it a point to visit, encourage, and support the bereaved in those weeks immediately after a funeral. (If the bereaved is a woman, the pastor's wife *must* go with him.) People are more vulnerable then than perhaps any other time. They need godly counsel. They need spiritual strength. They need a pastor perhaps more than at any other time in life. It is a crucial time of re-adjustment to life and the absence of their loved one.

5. Be a friend to the people. A pastor will rise to the pulpit and thunder forth the Word of God. He will stand in a Sunday School class and teach the deep things of the Word of God. He will oversee various meetings of groups within the church. These certainly are all part of the ministry and oversight of the church. However, a pastor needs to be a friend to his people. My father always had an open-door policy. Unless he was counseling or involved with some other confidential meetings, his study door was usually ajar. People knew they could drop by, knock, and come in for a chat, prayer, or whatever. At his funeral, numerous men made it a point to say he was the best friend they ever had.

Look for ways to show friendship to the people. Part of this is integrated into a policy of attempting to visit in the homes of the people. People need a visit when there is a crisis in the family. If there are notable absences from the services, either the pastor or someone from the church should seek to visit the absentee. When there are problems, the pastor should go deal with the trouble. It seems how truly the squeaky wheel gets the most attention. However, there are the stable, faithful, steadfast people who have few problems, are never absent, and rarely face crises in their lives. They tend to never be visited by the pastor. Dad tried to visit even the 'inner circle' of the church every now and then and have prayer with them. He looked for excuses to show up.

If someone has built a new house, it is good for the pastor to drop in and "inspect" the new house. People are always proud of their new home (even if it isn't actually new). Similarly, if someone had remodeled their house or added a room, it became an occasion for the pastor to drop in and check it out. If one of the men in the church has caught a trophy fish and had it mounted, it might merit a visit by the pastor to admire. A new deer head on the wall, or some new trophy are reasons to give people attention. These things may not seem to have any great spiritual value. But showing attention to the little achievements of the people is a big deal to them. Moreover, such attention builds a bond between people and pastor, which makes, them more amenable to counsel from the pulpit. It squelches the embers of grumbling or undercurrents of discontent before they ever get started. In short, it helps to build a stronger bond between the people in the pew and their pastor. In so doing, the overall ministry of the church is strengthened and stabilized.

There were many, many times the pastor met with men from the church at some coffee shop for a bite, fellowship, and prayer. He understood the importance of being a friend to his people. It paid off in a ministry which lasted for decades in one place. It may have been a lonely trucker home off the road for a few days. It may have been the small businessman struggling to keep his business afloat. It may have been the husband his pastor knew was having trouble at home, or the parent who was having difficulty with his children. Their pastor tried to help his people by being a friend to them. When people came to the office for formal counseling, the tone was more that of a friend than of a therapist.

6. Never embarrass people. The last five thoughts have been positive in nature. However, at times, it is crucial negative matters be avoided. As I have observed the ministry for more than a quarter of a century, it has amazed me how some pastors have little compunction about openly embarrassing or reprimanding their people. The relationship of people to their church is voluntary. They don't have to come. They don't have to be involved. In a church, people come and get involved because they desire to do so. There is no compulsion for them to attend. They voluntarily choose to do so.

Foolish however is a pastor who takes his people for granted. Though they may have been around for a long time and even very much involved, they can always leave. Every pastor has experienced that. It never is pleasant, even when the departing one is a problem. However, sometimes it is the pastor who is the problem. I think of several situations over the years where pastors have taken their people for granted by embarrassing them or unduly reprimanding them.

I will call him Pastor Westman. He had been the pastor of the church for four years. The honeymoon was over. But by now, he knew the church, the community, and the people. He had become comfortable and was well settled into his position. He took for granted his influence of leadership. He was the pastor, and he ran the program. He sensed a particular area of the church needed to be strengthened, so he planned a new program to stimulate interest therein. He asked a mature individual in the church to take charge of the program and build it. The man responded enthusiastically and plans were promoted. At the second meeting of this group, the appointed layman rose to conduct it. In the course of the program, he said something which the pastor did not favor. Rather than wait until after the meeting to privately talk to the man, Pastor Westman rose on the spot and announced that they were not going to do thus and thus. It was not a matter of doctrine, principle, or compromise. It was just something the pastor did not like.

In so doing, he *publicly* embarrassed this well-meaning layman. Maybe the man should have come to the pastor first and enquired whether the pastor would support this. But at times laymen do not always address things in the proper way. However, Pastor Westman created an even greater faux pas. He had humiliated a man in his church who only was trying to do what he thought was best. As a consequence of that incident (1) this layman resigned his leadership

Help the People!

of that program. (2) The program fell apart never to be restarted. (3) Within several months, this man and his wife left the church. He had lost confidence in his pastor. Maybe he had flubbed in not clearing a matter with his pastor first. However, he could not understand how the pastor would so embarrass him publicly. (4) Those present witnessing the debacle lost a degree of esteem for their pastor. One thing I learned from my father was to never publicly embarrass people. If there was a matter to be corrected, it ought to be done privately behind closed doors. Even then, he would be gracious in the matter.

I am mindful of another incident wherein a pastor openly reprimanded people in the church. Pastor Jaros was young in the ministry. He held strong convictions about certain things. When people in the church did not measure up to his convictions, Pastor Jaros had the tendency to jump them about it. He believed women who had shorter hair were compromising with the world. One day a young woman in his church got a new hairdo. The beautician had inadvertently cut off more than she expected. She wound up with a moderately short hairdo. It was not her intention. It just was the way it turned out. After the morning service the next Sunday, Pastor Jaros reprimanded her in the foyer of the church. There were other people present and heard him lecture her on having a worldly hairdo. Whether one agrees with that particular position is beside the point. The point is, this pastor foolishly embarrassed this woman before others. She was humiliated. Not surprisingly, she and her family left the church shortly thereafter. Without regard to his position, the pastor should never have openly embarrassed her.

Henry Sorenson held very conservative standards and convictions. However, he rarely confronted people about their failure to adhere to those standards. If anything was ever said, it usually was done by preaching the biblical principle undergirding a conviction from the pulpit. It was never obvious he was trying to straighten someone out. He scrupulously avoided making application to any

The Art of Pastoring

individual in the church who might be weak in that area. Rather, he preached biblical principles and encouraged people to comply.

The greater over-arching principle was to help and encourage the people. If he drove them away, he would not have the long-term prospect of ministering to them. He patiently taught, admonished, and led by example. People on occasion need to be rebuked and convicted of wrong. However, such reproof will be much better received if they know their pastor loves them and has had an established track record of seeking to help them. A cowboy will drive his herd. A shepherd will lead his flock. Help and encourage the people. They will respond over the long run.

Chapter Five - Preach the Word!

"Preach the word: be instant in season, out of season"

If there is one matter which is central to being a pastor, it is the preaching and teaching of God's Word. The focal point where most people see and hear their pastor is in the pulpit preaching the Word of God. The love and care of a pastor will emanate from the pulpit as much if not more than any other forum. The pulpit becomes the sacred desk to which a godly pastor will carefully and prayerfully rise each week. Perhaps in more than any other ministry he performs, the Spirit of God *can* fill and anoint him with power as he preaches.

Preaching has always been emphasized through the Bible. The ministry of the Word has been central to God's work throughout recorded history. During the Old Testament, the preacher was variously noted as a prophet, priest, and some cases king. For example, the psalmist wrote, *"I have **preached** righteousness in the great congregation: lo I have not refrained my lips,"* (Psalm 40:9). The prophet Isaiah wrote, *"The Spirit of the Lord God is upon me; because the Lord hath anointed me to **preach** good tidings unto the* *meek,"* (Isaiah 61:1). Jesus applied that reference directly to Himself in Luke 4. God commissioned the prophet Jonah to *"Arise, go unto Nineveh, that great city, and **preach** unto it the preaching that I bid thee,"* (Jonah 3:2). In the New Testament Paul wrote, *"And how shall they hear without a preacher? . . . How beautiful are the feet of them that **preach** the gospel of peace, and bring glad tidings of good things!"* (Romans 10:14-15). In writing to the church at Colosse, Paul said, *"Whom we **preach**, warning every man, and teaching every man in all wisdom; that we may present every man perfect in Christ Jesus,"* (Colossians 1:28).

In the New Testament, the primary focal point of ongoing preaching has been focused through the pastor in his pulpit. Therefore, Paul wrote to Timothy, *"**Preach the word.**"* The concept of preaching is noted at least 135 times in the New Testament. Paul wrote Titus how God *"hath in due times manifested his word through **preaching**,"* (Titus 1:3).

Teaching God's Word is closely related. A closely corresponding concept is the matter of teaching. For example, in the Great Commission, Jesus commanded us to be *"**teaching** them to observe all things whatsoever I have commanded you,"* (Matthew 28:20). The early church did exactly that: *"daily in the temple, and in every house, they ceased not to **teach and preach** Jesus Christ,"* (Acts 5:42). Paul spent at least 18 months in Corinth *"**teaching** the word of God among them"* (Acts 18:11). The last verse in the book of Acts notes how Paul spent his time in Rome *"**preaching** the kingdom of God, **and teaching** those things which concern the Lord Jesus Christ, with all confidence,"* (Acts 28:31). One of the qualities for a pastor is that he be *"apt to **teach**,"* (I Timothy 3:2). The matter of teaching appears slightly more than half as much as the matter of preaching in the New Testament. However, in the pastoral epistles (written as guidelines for pastoring), there is considerably more emphasis laid upon teaching than preaching. Paul said "preach the Word" once to Timothy. However, there are at least six direct references in Timothy and Titus to teaching the Word of God.

Preach the Word!

In the New Testament, there are at least ten references where both teaching and preaching appear in the same verse. One clear example is in Acts 15:35 where Luke notes how *"Paul also and Barnabas continued in Antioch, **teaching and preaching** the word of the Lord, with many others also."* One thing is for sure. Both teaching and preaching the Word of God is clearly taught throughout the Scripture, particularly in the context of the local church.

Ministering to the mind as well as the heart. Teaching is fundamentally a ministry to the mind. It is illuminating and expounding truth so one's mind can gain knowledge and understanding of God's Word. In contrast, preaching is primarily a ministry to the heart. The heart is the seat of the human spirit. It is the control room of our lives. There resides our will. There the basic decisions of life are made. Preaching will influence our heart to do as we ought to do or be as we ought to be. It may be the gospel in which God's Word along with the Holy Spirit persuades an individual to turn to Christ and trust Him as Savior. Or, it may be the preaching of righteousness which persuades a sinner to live unto righteousness. Both are ministries of the Word. Both are remanded to the custody of the church. Both are ministries a pastor is commanded to do. Both are of necessity, yea vital importance.

II Timothy 4:2

One of the most poignant portions of the New Testament is found in II Timothy 4. It has been called, among other things, Paul's swan song. It is his pathos-filled portent of impending martyrdom. Not only was there profound tragedy as the great apostle soon faced the executioner's blade, the circumstances of his martyrdom were truly poignant. He wrote from the Mamartine prison in Rome. No longer was he under house arrest as in the last seven chapters of Acts. Now, he was imprisoned in a literal dungeon awaiting death. It was little more than a hole in the ground, not unlike a sewer.

It is not hard to detect the heartfelt disappointment as Paul writes. In the hour of his greatest crisis, he wrote *"Demas hath forsaken me, having loved this present world,"* (verse 10). Other associates for whatever reason had bailed out. Only his faithful companion in travel, Luke, was with him in Rome. The greatest missionary of all time lay languishing in a Roman dungeon. He pathetically begged Timothy to come visit and bring his cloak which had been left at Troas. The weather was getting cold, and the subterranean dungeon obviously was chilly and damp. No one in Rome cared. He went on to note how at his first hearing (before Nero), no one stood with him. Where Luke was is not noted. However, in his hour of need, not one Christian would put his neck on the line and stand with Paul. He notes tragically how *"all men forsook me"* (verse 16). Moreover, he prayed such failure *"would not be laid to their charge."* He then went on to note how at his first hearing, he was *"delivered out of the mouth of the lion"* (verse 17). Though Paul was spared being thrown to the lions at Rome, he not long thereafter was executed. Though the Scripture does not leave an inspired record of his death, other history records Nero had him beheaded.

Though Paul, in writing to Timothy, did not know exactly how or when his death would take place, he knew it was near. With all of this in view he wrote Timothy, *"I am now ready to be offered, and the time of my departure is at hand. I have fought a good fight, I have finished my course, I have kept the faith"* (verses 6-7). (The word translated *offered* {spendo} has the sense of being poured out.)

Paul's final imperatives. With that poignant backdrop, Paul concluded his epistle to Pastor Timothy with several imperatives. (We will look at only the first several for our purposes in this chapter.) These imperatives are just as salient for pastors today as they were for Timothy then. With his end near, Paul used a term which is just as somber. He said, *"I charge thee therefore before God, and the Lord Jesus Christ who shall judge the quick and the dead at his appearing and his kingdom,"* (verse 1). The word

Preach the Word!

translated *charge* (diamarturomai) is a word from the judicial world. It literally means "to solemnly testify." In modern vernacular, it might be likened to one upon the witness stand "solemnly swearing" to tell the truth. Paul, like a judge behind the bar of justice, essentially issued an injunction to Timothy. Like a judge issuing an injunction in a grave situation, he *charged* Timothy. The idea is forceful, and like a court order, one which cannot be ignored.

To add further gravity to the injunctions about to be issued, Paul noted the other august parties present in the courtroom. Witnessing that which he was about to enjoin this young pastor was the appellate court of God the Father and the Lord Jesus Christ. With that awesome bench of Justices taking note of the proceedings, the great apostle under the inspiration of the Holy Spirit enjoined Pastor Timothy to "*preach the word*." For the record, the verb *preach* (kerusso) is presented in the imperative mode. It is an order from God, via the inspiration of the Holy Spirit, to pastors both then and now. We are enjoined to preach His Word! That is, we are under an injunction from the highest court to so preach.

Sadly, untold "reverends" rise to their pulpit week after week to deliver messages of political action, usually liberal in nature (though sometimes, conservative). To that are added homilies of social justice and social action. Sermons of philosophy, altruism, and humanism are common. Many rise to deliver discourses on the latest pop-psychological fad. It may be a big-deal about the power of positive thinking, or some related upbeat, feel-good, pep talk. It may be intoning the need for building positive self-esteem. But whatever, modern clergy in mainline denominations rarely exposit the Book of Books other than reading a text out of context to lend credence to their own ideas. This author has attended funerals officiated by modern clergy who not only never cracked the Book, but did not even allude to God other than an oblique mention to some great white spirit in the sky.

The Art of Pastoring

Content

Exposit the content of the Word of God. Our charge as pastors is to preach the Word! There is a profound need for Bible-believing pastors to preach the Word of God and **its content**. There is a dearth across the land of genuine exegesis of the Scripture resulting in accurate exposition of God's Word. The term "expository preaching" means a number of things to varying groups across the land. To some, the term "expository preaching" denotes a dry, professorial, systematic, line-upon-line, precept-upon-precept manner of preaching. However, by expositional preaching, I mean preaching what the Book actually says. It is rising to the sacred desk and in effect thundering forth, "Thus saith the Lord!" Technically, expository preaching is developing a passage of Scripture and preaching it in distinction to presenting a truth topically, or focusing solely upon a given text. However, in a broader sense, both topical and textual preaching can be expositional. The greater truth is to preach what the Word of God says. The form of the homiletic is not what is crucial. The content is.

So much preaching is merely taking a pet subject and nailing on several texts to add a pretense of being scriptural. Preaching preconceived notions buttressed by a text or two (sometimes out of context) is not preaching the Word. It is strikingly similar to what the cults do. Exegesis is extracting from the Word what it actually says and means. Eisegesis is reading into a text what one wishes it to mean, hoping to support a preconceived position. Even worse, is preaching which mimics what Dr. So-and-so believes. Our charge is to preach the Word, not what another famous preacher may preach.

Fresh messages are like a freshly cooked meal. Our preaching needs to be fresh and that can happen only as the preacher goes to the Book each week and extracts truth therefrom to be presented to the church. I marvel at the various advertisements I from time to time see, offering pastors pre-canned sermons and ready-to-go outlines. In the course of the ministry, there may come weeks when an ox falls in the ditch, and the pastor genuinely did not have time to adequately prepare. However, a pastor which would rely on such canned fodder should not be in the pulpit on a regular basis. Our charge is to preach the Word, not someone else's pre-cooked entré. On rare occasions, this author has had the misfortune to eat a TV dinner or some other pre-concocted frozen fare. It never is as good as a simple, home-prepared meal cooked on the kitchen stove. In the view of this author, a plain, old-fashioned, homemade hamburger is better than the frozen, pop-in-the-oven entré. As a young preacher, I once was admonished by an old deacon for preaching a message out of the file cabinet. Something had gone wrong that week. There may have been some sort of emergency. But rather than prepare a message from scratch, I pulled one from the file cabinet. The old deacon likened that to warming leftovers rather than freshly cooked food. He was right. There may be occasions when such is a necessity. But the charge for pastors remains to preach the Word, not a sermon outline, whatever its source.

Context

If the pastor does not provide understanding of biblical context, who will? Not only does the Word of God need to be preached in its content, but also its context. This touches perhaps more upon teaching the Word of God, but nevertheless, it is needful. On occasion, systematic teaching of the Bible may not always be dynamic and exciting. Portions of the Old Testament or Paul's dealing with Judaism in the New Testament may not be the mountain peak portions of Scripture in the view of many. Yet, it still is the Word of God.

The local church is God's ordained ground and pillar of the truth. If a local church does not teach the full spectrum of biblical knowledge, who will? God has ordained the local church to *teach them all things*, not para-church organizations. The focal point of such teaching comes back to the pastor. It is his job to either do the teaching himself or see to it others such as Sunday School teachers do. Paul wrote to Pastor Timothy, "*These things teach and exhort,*" (I Timothy 6:2).

Connection

A pastor must preach on the level where his people live. This leads us to the next thought, and that is to preach the Word in **its connection**. The people in the pew live in the real world. Every one of them face problems. All of them have burdens. All of them are influenced by the world, the flesh, and the devil. Whether they are afflicted by temptation or discouragement, the preaching of the Word of God from the pulpit needs to meet the need in their lives. There needs to be a connection between what resides within the covers of the Sacred Volume and where the people live. That connection must be made by the pastor as he preaches. Therefore, a pastor must preach the Word in such a way the needs and problems of the people are met. Whether it be evangelism, encouragement, exhortation, or edification, it is our job in the pulpit to take the endless resources of God's truth and apply it to the need of the person in the pew.

There frequently will be unsaved people visiting services. Though the local church is a body of believers, nevertheless, it is the opinion of this author how the gospel of salvation be preached and an invitation to receive Christ be presented in every service. There often are people who have slid back into sin or the world. Preaching must connect the Word of God to their hearts to convict them of their need of repentance. There are always people in the pew who have need of encouragement. There are always Christians who need to be stirred to serve God. Therefore, a pastor must preach in such a way as to connect the myriad of promises of God's Word to those who are discouraged. He needs to preach the Book in such a way the careless are stirred to be as they ought to be and do as they ought to do.

Preach the Word!

A pastor must always be prepared to preach. The apostle then added what perhaps is a parenthetical thought for Timothy. (By parenthetical, we mean the thought is adjunct to the main flow of the developing point.) Paul told Pastor Timothy to *"be instant in season, out of season."* The word translated *"be instant"* (ephistemi) has the sense "to be prepared" or "to be ready." It derives from the idea "to stand-by." It also is one of the imperatives of Paul's charge to Pastor Timothy. The phrases *"in season, out of season"* are of interest. The first - "in season" - literally could be translated "good time." The last - "out of season" - literally means "no time." In other words, we are charged to be prepared to preach when it is a good time to do so, and when it is not a good time. The greater thought is be prepared - prepared in content, prepared in prayer, prepared to open our mouths boldly as we ought on any occasion. It is not difficult to be prepared for the proper time such as the Sunday morning service. But we also need to be prepared when it is not easy. It may be a difficult funeral. The gospel needs to be preached nevertheless. It may be bearing down on sin or other problems. It seems there is never an easy time to do so. Yet, Paul charged Pastor Timothy to be prepared when the time was good and the circumstances were easy. But he also charged him (and us by extension) to be prepared to preach when the occasion is trying and the circumstances are difficult. Be instant in season, out of season!

Reprove, Rebuke, Exhort

Continuing, the Holy Spirit through Paul developed a pattern for pastoral preaching. He urged Pastor Timothy to (1) reprove, (2) rebuke, and (3) exhort. Again, each of these action-packed verbs are imperatives. It is therefore incumbent upon us to examine exactly what the Holy Spirit intended in so charging us.

Let us look more closely at these injunctions. There actually is a progression of thought in the three imperatives. The first is the most stern and the last the most cheering. The thought spectrum therefore ranges from essentially scolding to encouraging.

Preach with the convicting power of the Holy Spirit. The first imperative - **reprove** - is translated from the word "elencho." It is the word most usually connected with the idea of conviction. The idea is to convict (in some cases with the thought of putting the convicted person to shame). It is the same word used regarding the Holy Spirit's conviction of sin, righteousness, and judgment in John 16:8. (*"And when he is come, he will reprove the world of sin, and of righteousness, and of judgment."*) The English word "convict," as it is usually used in a spiritual context, basically means to "convince." Hence, when an individual is "convicted" of their sin, the idea is how they have become convinced and ashamed of their sin. Similarly, the ministry of the Holy Spirit is to reprove (i.e. convict or convince) of righteousness as well as judgment. Therefore, as the occasion arises, the Spirit of God will convince the hearts of men of what is right or of God's coming judgment.

In preaching the gospel, a heart consumed with a passion for the lost on the part of the preacher with the power of the Holy Spirit will convince the sinner of his need of salvation. In preaching righteousness, the conviction of the preacher can impart conviction in the heart of the hearer to do right. And similarly, in preaching of coming judgment, the conviction of the preacher can help impart the same to the hearer.

The preacher is merely a vehicle for the truth. He is simply a messenger. Whatever ability to convince on his part frequently is meager in attempting to pierce hardened hearts. There must be supernatural help in convincing hearts corrupted by sin to turn to the Savior. There must be help from heaven in convicting a backslider to return to fellowship. There must be divine assistance in entering hearts clouded over by the world, the flesh, and the devil. This is the needed ministry of the Spirit of God.

The human heart is a spiritual entity. It transcends our minds and emotions. The devil certainly can influence it in ways we do not fully understand. But the One who is greater can also influence the heart to repentance and faith. That One is the Holy Spirit. As God's Word is preached, it is the Holy Spirit who ultimately convinces the heart of its need, whether of salvation, repentance, or doing what is right. The instrument used by the Spirit is the Word of God. The messenger He utilizes is the preacher. Hence, as we preach the Word of God with commanded conviction, the Spirit can take that supernatural cutting edge to pierce hearts hardened by sin. I do not fully understand the mystery of how God allows sinful mankind to make the final decision to turn to Christ or turn away. But ours is not to understand. Ours is to obey. We are commanded in preaching to reprove. That is, it is our duty to convince of the spiritual need at hand. Whether the need is of salvation, repentance, or other spiritual decision, we are enjoined to convict the hearer. That, of course, is fully accomplished as the Spirit of God empowers the preacher and convicts the hearer by the Word of God.

Recall how preaching is a ministry largely to the heart. The seat of our will resides there. That is, decisions are made in the heart. Therefore, preaching ought to be directed to the heart with the aid of the convicting power of the Holy Spirit. Therefore, to reprove in preaching is a comprehensive process of a convicted, Spirit-filled preacher, preaching the Word of God, which the Spirit of God utilizes to convince the hearer. That conviction is intended to persuade the hearer to obey what the Holy Spirit has impressed upon him.

Preach to urge people to do as they ought. The next imperative - **rebuke** - is perhaps not as harsh as the English translation might imply. It is translated from "epitimao." That word is made up of two simpler words. The primary word is "timao" which basically means "to honor or to value." The prefix "epi" is a basic preposition with the sense of "on" or "upon." Literally, the word "epitimao" means to put honor or value upon. In time, it developed into the idea of judging in the sense of determining the value of whatever. It eventually became idiomatic of the idea to admonish or urge someone to do as they ought; that is, to live up to one's potential honor, or to do as they ought to do. The English word carries the sense of correcting by severely chiding a shirker. However, the Greek word has a more positive sense of urging an individual to do right, to do as they ought, or to do his best.

One illustration which comes to mind is that of a coach. He will exhort members of his team to do as they ought. He will urge them to play to their potential. He will not only instruct them, but he will goad them to do their best. And that is an injunction which is laid upon each New Testament pastor. In rising to the pulpit, we are enjoined among other things to urge our people to do as they ought to do. Recall how Jesus in the Great Commission enjoined us to be "*teaching them to observe all things whatsoever I have commanded you,*" (Matthew 28:20). That is, we are commanded to urge our people to *observe* or to *do* all things whatsoever He has commanded us.

Implied is the principle of righteousness. Though the principle of righteousness is not explicitly stated, it certainly is implied. In Psalm 40, the great messianic Psalm, Jesus Christ through David prophetically said, "*I have preached righteousness in the great congregation: lo, I have not refrained my lips, O LORD, thou knowest,*" (Palm 40:9). If we would be Christ-like in our ministry, here is one simple yet profound example. Our Lord's ministry certainly was one of urging those who heard His voice to do as they ought. To that degree, He was a preacher of righteousness. Interestingly, Noah likewise was called a preacher of righteousness (II Peter 2:5). In similar fashion, Jesus foretold how the Holy Spirit's ministry would in part be of convicting men of righteousness when He departed (John 16:10).

As noted above, Paul charged Pastor Timothy to not only convict men of their spiritual needs in preaching, but also urge them to live up to the righteous expectations God had set before them. The word is "rebuke." However, as we have seen, the sense of the underlying word is more to urge or admonish to do as one ought.

Once again, it is set forth as an imperative. The progression thus is (1) to reprove (i.e. convince of spiritual need), (2) to rebuke (i.e. to admonish to do right), and then (3) to exhort.

Preach to encourage. The third imperative, **exhort**, has an even gentler sense. It is translated from the Greek word "parakaleo." Once again, it is a compound verb made up of two more basic words. The primary root is "kaleo" which simply means "to call." The prefix "para" has the sense of "by," "along side of," or "near." The two together literally have the sense "to call to one's side" or "to summon." However, as is the case in all language, words usually develop a related sense apart from the most literal sense. The word "parakaleo" came to have the idea of drawing someone near to console them. A simple illustration might be of beckoning someone to encourage them. The greater idea is of "consoling" or "comforting." (Both those words are translated from "parakaleo" in the Authorized Version.) In practical usage, the word "parakaleo" came to have the modern sense of encouragement.

In the view of this author, Paul charged Pastor Timothy to encourage his people. That charge remains to this day. The truth is, people sitting under the preaching of the Word more often than not carry burdens. They face pressures of modern life. There is stress in their lives. It may be financial worry. It may be trouble at work. It may be the prospect of down-sizing or layoff. The businessman may be experiencing a difficult year. There may be trouble at home. A marriage may be in a state of a cold war or even worse. There may be heartaches with children. There may be health concerns. There is no end to the problems people carry on their shoulders as they walk through the door of the church building each Sunday. To be sure, there is a need for reprimanding sin. There is a need to prod God's people to do more. But there always is a need to encourage them. People need to be reminded of the promises of God. They need to be brought back to the mercy and grace of God as it pertains to day-to-day Christian living. They need to be refreshed in how God delivered and supplied His people in days gone by.

Be a Blessing to the People

Preaching to bless the people is not only virtuous in its own merit, it prepares the way for harder preaching. My father would say to me, "Son, bless the people when you get up to preach." At the time, I did not fully understand that advice. Today, I do. People come to a preaching service for any number of reasons. For some, it is out of a sense of duty and faithfulness. They will be there regardless of what is delivered from the pulpit. Others come seeking to be edified or to grow in grace. Others come for less spiritual reasons such as habit, family, or social reasons. But regardless of the motive for their presence, people will respond to being blessed. Not only is it an expression of loving the people, it is very practical as well. When people are encouraged and blessed by their pastor, they become more willing to receive messages of scolding or admonishment. When they know their pastor loves them and has their best interest at heart, he can rise to the pulpit and urge them to do what they ought to do, and they will be much more responsive. In the view of this author, there ought to be more preaching of encouragement than of chastisement or admonishment. The reason is simple. People will respond better to messages urging them to shape up or do as they ought when the pastor has encouraged them, blessed them, and lifted them up. Then, he can bear down upon them if need be. However, if his preaching is predominantly sharp, focusing on short-comings or problems, people become resistant to it. It can lead to hardening of hearts, at least toward him.

"With all Longsuffering and Doctrine"

Exhort with patience. It is noteworthy how this third imperative (exhort) is the only one which has additional explanation. Paul embellished this thought by noting how such exhortation (i.e. encouragement) ought to be *"with all longsuffering and doctrine."* Let us look at each of these qualities.

The Holy Spirit used two words in the New Testament which have the sense of patience or longsuffering. The one, "hupomone," has more of the idea of "perseverance" or "stick-to-i-tive-ness." The other, "makrothumia," has more to do with "being patient with people." It bespeaks bearing with them and putting up with them. The latter is the word used by Paul here. As we preach, the Holy Spirit has admonished us to be patient with those to whom we minister. The greater idea is to patiently encourage those whom God has given us the privilege to pastor. They need it. God often has been patient with us. We likewise need to be longsuffering in our preaching to those whom we would encourage.

Exhort with doctrine. Finally, our exhortation ought to be with all doctrine. The word translated "doctrine" simply means teaching. That essence of course is the truth - *"thy word is truth."* Paul went on to note in verses 3 and 4, the time was fast approaching when sound doctrine would be corrupted. The practical outworking is how pastoral preaching ought to have an element of teaching. Not only ought God's people to know what they ought to do, but why. They need to be taught. If the pastor of a local church does not teach the Word of God to his people, they either (a) will not be grounded, or, (b) someone else will teach them. It is reported that a high percentage of "converts" made by both the Jehovah's Witnesses and the Mormons are ungrounded Baptists. The cults prey and focus upon spiritually feeble Baptists whose pastors have never taken the time to teach them the Word of God.

Moreover, as those in the pew understand the Word of God, its promises become of greater encouragement. As we grow in the grace *and the knowledge* of our Lord Jesus Christ, we grow to the point where we henceforth are no more *"children, tossed to and fro, and carried about with every wind of doctrine."* Paul charged Pastor Timothy to teach his people as he reproved, rebuked, and exhorted.

In summary, Paul charged Timothy, and by extension every pastor since, to preach the Word. That involves being prepared whether it is a good time or not. It is convincing the people of the

The Art of Pastoring

truth. It is admonishing them to do as they ought, living up to the righteous standard God has established for them. And then, it is patiently encouraging the people, teaching them the "whys" and "wherefores" of God's Word.

Meet the Needs of the People

Having examined Paul's instructions to Pastor Timothy, let us make further comment concerning pastoring and preaching. A pastor ought to seek to meet the needs of his people as he prepares and delivers messages from the pulpit. Those needs will be diverse in nature. They will range from strengthening areas of doctrinal weaknesses to meeting the needs of people in their day-to-day problems.

Preach to strengthen biblical doctrine. As a pastor perceives doctrinal areas in the church which need shoring up, he ought to address them from the pulpit. A current refrain heard in some circles is how doctrine ought to be down-played. It is alleged that doctrine is boring. It doesn't meet the needs of people where they live. Moreover, it is alleged, doctrine is divisive. The claim is made, it divides the body of Christ. The fact of the matter is, sound doctrine is the framework for properly understanding God's Word. A well-prepared preacher can make even the deepest of biblical doctrine fascinating - and he ought. To the allegation doctrine divides, the rejoinder is simple. Doctrine only divides truth from error. It would seem the enemy has fostered this foolishness in the hope undiscerning preachers will avoid any emphasis thereon. Paul charged Pastor Timothy to preach the word . . . with all doctrine.

The word "doctrine" as previously noted literally means "teaching." As we have used the word at this point, the greater sense is the systematic body of truth which comprises Bible teaching. If the people in the pew do not learn the great doctrines of inspiration, the blood atonement, the deity of Christ, the virgin birth, the Trinity, and much more from their pastor, where are they going to learn? Either

Preach the Word!

they will remain spiritually ignorant of these foundational truths, becoming easy prey for a cult, or someone else will teach them. It may be a radio or TV preacher. It may be tapes they get a hold of. It may be literature they happen upon. A pastor who does not preach doctrine to his people is inviting spiritual disaster for them sooner or later.

Getting back to the idea of meeting the needs of the people, as a pastor becomes aware of doctrinal weaknesses, he ought to preach to strengthen those areas. For example, a young convert in the church was zealous in his witnessing at work. He quickly found some of his co-workers were Jehovah's Witnesses who proceeded to cross-examine him about the deity of Christ. He came and asked his pastor the "whys" and "wherefores" of the Jehovah's Witnesses and why the deity of Christ was important. That became a signal for the pastor to begin to preach several messages concerning not only the deity of Christ, but also other doctrinal issues the JW's like to pounce upon. The truth is, if one person in the church is having doctrinal problems, that is reason enough to preach on the matter. Moreover, there no doubt are others who are weak at that point.

One reason the charismatic movement has made such inroads over the past generation is people have not heard good preaching about the Holy Ghost. Pentecostals and charismatics are quick to point out particularly to young Christians how they haven't experienced the full joy of being saved until they have had some charismatic experience. They imply others don't have the whole of salvation. It sounds very enticing to young believers. Sound preaching on the Holy Spirit will stave off much of the charismatic confusion with which so many Christians have been confounded.

Areas of separation, be they personal or ecclesiastical, are rooted in biblical doctrine, particularly the matter of holiness and obedience. These need to be preached, especially as a pastor perceives such to be a problem within his church. We are enjoined to preach doctrine. Our duty is to sense or perceive areas within our congregation which are weak in this regard and strengthen our people lest they be carried about with some wind of doctrine. If we do not ground them, the devil may waft some enticing aroma of false doctrine before them.

Preach to meet the perceived needs of the church. There is a never-ending need to develop God's people in their spiritual growth. In any given service, there will always be a wide spectrum of spiritual maturity. Some are relatively young Christians. Others grew up in the church but have never grown much spiritually. Others have slid back into carnality. Preaching aimed at stirring the heart to greater spiritual growth is always needed. A perceptive pastor will perceive particular needs within his church. They may stem from counseling sessions. They may come from casual conversation. They may come thru the grapevine. But if a pastor is perceptive to what is going on in his church, he will frequently be aware of spiritual weaknesses in his people. These therefore become areas from which he can plan his preaching. He ought not enter the pulpit to "grind an ax" or attack problem people. However, if one of his people have a particular weakness, the chances are more have the same need. He therefore can enter the pulpit to deal with principles directed to strengthen the area of need.

As noted earlier, my father used to say to me, "Son, bless the people when you preach." By that he did not mean sin or problems should be ignored. What he did realize after decades in the pulpit is how people probably need more encouragement than they get. Messages which teach a great truth will bless. Messages which lift up Jesus bless. Messages concerning heaven and the hope of glory bless people. Messages which reveal great truths such as grace, salvation, and faith can be tools for great blessing for God's people.

Preach to strengthen the people. There is a great deal in the Bible about strength. The Book of Psalms redounds with passages dealing with how God gives strength and, in fact, is the source of strength Himself. For example, in Psalm 27:1, the psalmist wrote how *"the LORD is the strength of my life."* And in Psalm 28:7, *"The LORD is my strength."* In Psalm 18:39, David wrote how *"thou hast girded* *me with strength unto the battle."* The people in the pew often are running on near-empty in their spiritual and emotional strength. Reminding them in preaching how *"they that wait upon the* LORD *shall renew their strength"* is always apropos. Reminding them of God's precious promises of provision will strengthen. Reminding them of His promised presence and His soon return strengthens. There always is a place for strengthening the people in pastoral preaching. It ought to be a regular part of the starting line-up of a pastor's rotation of messages.

Preach against sin. In contrast, a perceptive pastor will soon be aware of sin in the lives of his people. It is a need and problem which seems endless. Whether they be overt sins of commission or the more pervasive sins of omission, there never is an end of sin to be preached against. It well may be sins of the flesh which usually are obvious. Less obvious, but probably more prevalent are sins of the spirit such as pride, stubbornness, and disobedience. Moreover, there always are Christians who are not doing as they ought. Faithfulness to the things of God is a perennial failing. Some don't tithe. Others won't witness. It all, quite frankly, is sin. Ought a pastor preach against such sin? Absolutely! It is a part of perceiving and meeting the needs of the people. Such preaching, as a rule, is not as well appreciated, but it is necessary nevertheless.

Preach principles, not personalities. A wise pastor will learn to be careful in dealing with problems. He will learn to deal with the *principle* of the problems and avoid the *personalities* involved. As people sense they are being targeted from the pulpit, they often pull back into their shell or rebel. Rather than preaching an entire message on a given problem, a wise pastor will "weave" the problem area to be addressed into the greater fabric of a less pointed message. Dad would often "weave" what had to be said into a more generic type of sermon. People got the point without getting their hackles up.

Though there is never a problem with encouraging people from the pulpit, we must be very careful about publicly chastening or rebuking. It usually does not take a rocket scientist to figure out who the pastor has in mind. More damage than good can result from such narrowly focused messages. I well remember the advice of an old preacher years ago, "Never grind an ax in the pulpit."

Plan your Preaching

Address the needs of the people. The question therefore arises - how a pastor should plan his preaching? What is the criteria of planning in sermon preparation? Any pastor who has been in the pulpit for any length of time knows that periodically there comes the time to prepare a message, and all he can draw is a blank. Some advocate a systematic through-the-book approach for message preparation. I once knew a pastor who prided himself on how he was preaching systematically through the Bible. Each week he preached sequentially chapter by chapter through the Bible.

I would suggest that might be a more appropriate approach for *teaching* the Bible. There is always a need for further systematic knowledge of the Word of God. However, in the view of this author, systematically preaching chapter by chapter is not the best way to approach the pulpit and sermon preparation. I heard a preacher years ago use the analogy of an apothecary regarding the Scripture and message preparation. He likened the Word of God to an apothecary of spiritual medicine. Indeed, the Scripture contains what is necessary for every need of the human heart. A physician will not prescribe his patient to go to the pharmacy and take the first pills on the shelf this week, then the next pills next week and so forth. Rather, a wise physician will seek to diagnose the need of his patient and then prescribe what is needed from the pharmacy.

Likewise, a wise pastor will seek to diagnose the spiritual needs of his people. He then will go to the pharmacy of the Word of God and present the appropriate spiritual medicine as the occasion requires. It may be the balm of Gilead. It may be the waters of Marah. It may be the milk of the Word. It may be the stimulant of hope. But whichever it is, God's Word has the answer. The job of the pastor is to sense the pulse of his congregation, perceive their spiritual temperature, and appropriately deliver what is required each Lord's day.

We are enjoined to preach the Word. What a great privilege! It becomes a blessing as a pastor goes to the Book of Books to find the requisite needs for his people. As he delivers the Word of God to them each week, meeting their spiritual needs, he serves both them and His Lord.

Chapter 6 -
Do the Work of an Evangelist!

"I was not disobedient unto the heavenly vision."

In continuing to examine the sequence of imperatives with which Paul charged Timothy, let us look at another command in II Timothy 4. We shall take the liberty to consider a crucial matter out of its textual sequence. However, we will complete the list of imperatives in coming chapters. In the same injunction Paul charged Timothy to preach the Word, he also charged him to do the work of an evangelist. In more modern parlance, we might paraphrase the command to be a soul winner.

As noted in an earlier chapter, God has established the office of evangelist (Ephesians 4:11) along with pastors and teachers. It is a specific calling. It is a gift from God to local churches. It continues to this day. However, here God did not call Timothy to *be* an evangelist in the sense of his overall calling. Rather, he charged him to *do the work* of an evangelist. In other words, the Holy Spirit charged Timothy to engage himself in the matter of winning people to Christ. He was a pastor. That was his primary calling.

Nevertheless, God commanded Timothy to *do the work* of an evangelist, to bring people to Christ, to win the lost, to evangelize.

Soul Winning is Commanded

We are commanded to evangelize. By all accounts, that command remains for each and every biblical pastor. It is an imperative not only in its importance, but in the very grammar of the sentence. We are *commanded* to evangelize. In recent years, I have heard some say, "I do not have the gift of evangelism." The truth is, it is not a gift. It is a command. The sense of it being a gift is in how God has called some men to assist churches as vocational evangelists. But all are commanded to win the lost. It is not an option. It is not a suggestion. It is not an alternate form of ministry. It is a God-inspired command incumbent upon all Christians, and of all people, especially pastors. Some may be more gifted than others in their ability, skill, and experience. But the imperative remains.

As implied, winning people to Christ is work. It is time-consuming. It is energy-consuming. It is often not easy. It can leave one emotionally, if not spiritually weary. I fear one reason why more spiritual leaders do not win souls is that it in fact is work. It is one of the more difficult aspects of the ministry. It is far easier to sit in the office and study than go and knock on the door of a sinner. It is easier to preside over some committee meeting than try and reach someone who does not want to be reached. It is far easier to talk about the gospel than actually engage the battle. It is far easier to go to a preachers' meeting and talk about missions, than practice the heartbeat of missions in one's own neighborhood. It is work. Nevertheless, one command in the New Testament for pastors is to do the work of an evangelist.

Do the Work of an Evangelist!

The Example of Paul

Not disobedient to the heavenly vision. This imperative is amply illustrated throughout the New Testament. If there was one thing which clearly represented the life and ministry of Paul, it was his never-ending endeavor to turn men from darkness unto light. Even as Jesus Christ commissioned him on the road to Damascus, he was not disobedient to that heavenly vision. As he stood before Agrippa in Acts 26, he noted how He was sent *"to open their eyes, and to turn them from darkness to light, and from the power of Satan unto God that they may receive forgiveness of sins, and inheritance among them which are sanctified,"* (Acts 26:18). Paul, after many years of serving the King, added, *"Whereupon, O king Agrippa, I was not disobedient unto the heavenly vision,"* (Acts 26:19).

Whether it was in Damascus or in Caesar's court, Paul made Christ manifest in all places. In every city and in every place he went, he did the work of an evangelist. Moreover, in virtually every venue, he faced stiff opposition, often escaping by the skin of his teeth. In fact, many believe he actually died at Lystra, and God miraculously raised him up to complete his ministry. From city to city and synagogue to synagogue, in some cases door to door, Paul did the work of an evangelist. He preached salvation publicly. He witnessed to both small and great privately. Wherever and whenever, his focus was continuously upon winning men to Christ. He sought to win common, everyday people. He sought to win kings. He witnessed to everyone in between.

We are enjoined to do as he did. We today are not commissioned as apostles in the strictest sense of the term. However, we certainly can follow in the apostle's example in being a soul winner. On two occasions, Paul wrote the Corinthians *"Be ye followers of me,"* (I Corinthians 4:16, 11:1). The word used in both cases (mimetes) has the sense of mimicking or doing as he did. In both of the noted cases, the context is bringing the gospel to others. It therefore follows, we have been enjoined to do as he did.

The Example of Jesus

Jesus was a soul winner. Not only did Paul set an example for us in winning others, more importantly our Lord did. To say Jesus was a soul winner is an understatement. As noted in Matthew 9:35-36, He frequently went from city to village teaching and preaching the gospel of the kingdom with a heart moved with compassion. He won Andrew, Peter, Nathaniel, and Philip. He won the rest of His disciples one by one. He convinced Nicodemus to trust Him. Countless thousands heard Him and trusted Him as Savior.

Though we will never have the fullness of the Spirit He had, nevertheless He commissioned us to take the gospel to others. Matthew recorded, *"Go ye therefore, and teach all nations,"* (Matthew 28:19). The word translated "nations" is "ethnos" from which the English word "ethnic" derives. It means peoples. Mark wrote, *"Go ye into all the world, and preach the gospel to every creature,"* (Mark 16:15). John recorded him saying, *"As my Father hath sent me, even so send I you,"* (John 20:21). Luke wrote, *"And ye shall be witnesses unto me . . . unto the uttermost part of the earth,"* (Acts 1:8). In each case, the charge to bring the gospel to others is either set forth as an imperative or with the force of an imperative. The simple truth is, Jesus Christ has commanded us to evangelize, to win souls, to bring others to Him and disciple them. It has been said, the Great Commission of Jesus Christ is our license to preach.

Fulfilling the Great Commission certainly is sending missionaries across the sea. But it is also taking the gospel across the street. Many no doubt have seen the plaque on the inside of some church doors which says, "You are now entering your mission field." Truly, as we leave the church building each time, we enter the mission field all about us. God has commissioned the church to be a lighthouse. It is the view of this author how every member of the church ought to be a soul winner. Of all people, the pastor needs to lead by example.

The Example of the early Church

Daily they ceased not to teach and preach Jesus Christ. Not only is the command to win people to Christ clearly developed in the various accounts of the Great Commission, it is reiterated throughout the book of Acts. It is clearly implied in Acts 4:19 where Peter replied to the Sanhedrin, *"Whether it be right in the sight of God to hearken unto you more than unto God, judge ye."* They had commanded them to cease and desist. God had **commanded** them to witness.

In Acts 5:20, God sent an angel to the imprisoned disciples who said, *"Go, stand and speak in the temple to the people all the words of this life."* The verb translated "speak" is rendered in the imperative mode. The angel God sent **ordered** the beleaguered disciples to go again and preach Christ. Meanwhile, the angel had opened the prison doors and shooed them out. The next day, the disciples were promptly arrested again for preaching Christ. When confronted by the authorities, Peter responded, *"We ought to obey God rather than men,"* (Acts 5:29). Peter and the other disciples clearly understood their orders from God. The apostles were therefore beaten and released with another injunction to keep their mouths shut. However, they *"daily in the temple, and in every house ceased not to teach and preach Jesus Christ,"* (Acts 5:42).

After Saul of Tarsus was confronted by Christ on the road to Damascus, God spoke to Ananias that He had chosen him to *"bear my name before the Gentiles, and kings, and the children of Israel,"* (Acts 9:15). The rest of Chapter 9 and for that matter the rest of the book of Acts, exemplifies how Paul fulfilled those heavenly **orders**.

When the angel of the Lord appeared to Peter at Joppa in Acts 10:22, he informed him how God was sending him to Cornelius *"to hear words of thee."* What is clearly implied is how God had in effect

ordered him to go to Caesarea to witness Christ there. Peter **obeyed**. Upon arriving at Cornelius' home, Peter opened his mouth and began to witness Christ to those assembled. Notice in verse 42 how Peter noted *"he **commanded** us to preach unto the people, and to testify."* Peter clearly understood the Great Commission. Jesus had **commanded** him to preach and testify of Him. That **commandment** extends to this very day for every preacher of the gospel.

When Jesus appeared to Paul by a vision at Corinth, He admonished him to *"Be not afraid, **but speak**, and hold not thy peace,"* (Acts 18:9). The context clearly is of witnessing Christ. The admonition by Jesus once again is in the **imperative** mode.

In Acts 26:16-18, Paul revealed further details of what Jesus said to him as he lay prostrate on the ground on his way to Damascus. The Lord informed him how He had appointed him to be a witness in turning the gentiles to Christ. As Paul stood and gave his testimony before King Agrippa, he confessed, *"I was **not disobedient** unto the heavenly vision,"* (Acts 26:19). He proceeded, *"having therefore obtained help of God, I continue unto this day, witnessing both to small and great,"* (Acts 26:22). Paul clearly understood the **mandate** given him by the Lord Jesus to win others to Christ. We today have not received a *heavenly vision* to witness. We have a more sure word. God has given us His authoritative written Word which **commands** us to witness and win souls.

130 examples in Acts alone. In addition to the **imperatives** of winning others in the Great Commission, there are scores of examples of the early church fulfilling that **command**. In the book of Acts alone, there are more than 130 instances of the early church witnessing, preaching Christ, and winning others. Philip, for example, witnessed to and won the Ethiopian eunuch in Acts 8. Those who were scattered abroad at Stephen's martyrdom went everywhere preaching the Word. They were not the leadership of the church, rather the rank and file. The church at Antioch was evidently started by witnessing brethren who had been scattered there. Acquila and Priscilla witnessed to Apollos and won him to Christ. The whole of the book of Acts is one successive record of the gospel being witnessed to Jew and gentile, citizens and kings. It was the acts of the apostles as well as the rank and file of the church.

When Paul wrote to Timothy to do the work of an evangelist, there was clear precedent. The first generation of the early church had already fulfilled the command of Jesus Christ in taking the gospel to those around them. Now, Paul admonished Timothy as a pastor to keep doing that blessed work.

The Example of Henry Sorenson

A soul winner. If there was one thing which characterized the ministry of my father, he was a soul winner. From shortly after Dad was saved to his last week of life, he witnessed to small and great, telling the wonderful news of the saving grace of our Lord Jesus Christ. He always carried a pocket New Testament and used it frequently to lead people to Christ wherever he was.

The last week of his life was spent for the most part in the hospital. He had suffered a mild heart attack prior to a massive heart failure approximately one week later. During that week, he witnessed to numerous nurses and several roommates. As one nurse came to do her duties, Dad asked her if she knew she was on her way to heaven. She said, "no." Therefore, while she tended to him, he took her down the Romans road and led her to Christ. Several days after being admitted and stabilized, Dad began to witness to his roommate. He was a crusty old railroad man named Bob. As Bob lay on his hospital bed, and Dad on his, he led Bob down the Romans road. There on his hospital bed, Bob received Christ as his Savior. Several days later, Dad died. Right to the end, he did the work of an evangelist.

Early in his Christian life in the mid-1930's, my father became a soul winner. He worked at a downtown bank. There, he led co-workers to Christ before he went off to Bible college to prepare for the ministry. He taught a Sunday School class before beginning to preach. He sought to lead each in his class to Christ. One of the

The Art of Pastoring

fellows he led to Christ from his class went to Europe as a missionary and served there for fifty years.

Dr. Sorenson always gave an invitation from the pulpit for salvation at the close of every preaching service. As I sat under his preaching over the years, there frequently were people who came to Christ as he extended an altar call to receive Christ. I remember one fellow in particular who got saved under his preaching. This particular fellow's wife had gotten saved through one of the ladies in the church. She began to grow and became faithful to the services of the church. Because this particular lady and her husband were young adults and because that was the group which was my Sunday School class as an assistant pastor, I visited in the home from time to time. I will call him Bill (which was not his real name). I would go out on Saturday mornings to visit for my Sunday School class. When Jane (not her real name) would see me coming, she would just open the door and I would walk into the house without knocking. If Bill heard someone knock on Saturday morning, he (rightly) assumed it was someone from the church and would go and hide. He did not want to be witnessed to or invited to church. One day when I went to visit, I was told he was hiding behind the furnace in the basement. I could not reach him.

Well, one day through some special promotional effort at the church, Bill came to a service. As my father preached, he sat there nervously, under conviction. When the invitation was given at the close of the service, Bill slipped out of the pew and down the aisle. Someone sat down with him and he was wonderfully saved. Dad always gave an invitation to receive Christ.

Henry Sorenson was an avid golfer. Though he tried to instill that habit into his son, it never much took hold. Nevertheless, Dad would go golfing almost every weekday the weather was suitable. He would buy a season pass for a local public golf course. Then he would rise at the crack of dawn many a morning and be on the links by six o'clock. He would shoot nine holes and be home by 7:30 a.m. It was a combination of exercise, recreation, and a time to be alone with the Lord at the beginning of the day. As those who regularly golf know, there are numerous other people who follow a similar golf schedule. My father also would meet the various greens' keepers and golf course maintenance people at that hour. As he got to know those he often met in the morning, he would inevitably begin to witness to them. There were numerous early golfers and golf course personnel Dad led to Christ on the golf course. Even in his retirement years as he continued to play golf each morning, he led course maintenance people to Christ. He did the work of an evangelist.

As mentioned in an earlier chapter, my father was regular in visiting people in the hospital. He faithfully visited people of his congregation as they were hospitalized. In some cases, they were relatives of members of the church, but Dad visited them as well. He found such hospital visits to be a fruitful field for winning people to Christ. He had a knack for approaching people on a hospital bed, making small talk, winning their friendship, and then asking them if they knew the Lord. He then would proceed to pull out his ever-present pocket New Testament and present the gospel to them. He led many to Christ in such a fashion over the years. Another variation Dad frequently practiced in hospital visitation was to greet the person in the other bed. He would ask if they would like for him to pray for them as well. Most people on a hospital bed will welcome any amount of prayer any minister is willing to offer. After befriending them through such contact, Dad would ask if they knew for sure they were on their way to heaven. Over the years, he led many to Christ is such fashion.

Dr. Sorenson not only visited the people of his congregation, he made regular soul winning visits on people with whom he had some sort of contact. They may have visited a service. They may have been new to town. They may have been referred to him by someone else. But he was out all the time seeking to win people to Christ. One particular visit comes to mind. He had tried several times to visit a man and wife who had visited one of the services of the church. Dad would go to visit at conventional hours such as 7 o'clock in the evening. The lady of the house told him her husband was not home from work. After several such unsuccessful attempts, he inquired when he could be found. She told him he drove a truck, and didn't get home until after nine in the evening. Therefore, one evening Dad went to visit them again, this time at 9:30 in the evening. That indeed is an unconventional time to go soul winning. But he was finally able to find this man at home.

In sitting down with them, the pastor had the privilege of leading both Ron and Rose Thacker to Christ. Dad counseled them how they needed to come to church Sunday and make public their profession of faith. They did come, but did not walk the aisle. In fact, they did not come back. However, about a year later, the Holy Spirit convicted Ron and Rose how they needed to become faithful. Ron and his wife began to attend regularly, were baptized, and he particularly began to witness zealously. In fact, as a layman in the church, Ron Thacker adopted the little slogan of winning a soul a day. He endeavored to do it and often succeeded. Not long thereafter, God called him to preach. He went off to Bible college, graduated, and has pastored for almost a quarter of a century. He along with scores of others went out into the ministry under my fathers's influence. But it all began because the pastor was a soul winner. He did the work of an evangelist.

As people would come to Dad's study from time to time for counsel, Dad would seize on the opportunity to witness to them if he thought they were not saved. On occasion, a young couple would wander in seeking a pastor and church in which to be married. Dr. Sorenson would pounce on such an opportunity like a bird on a bug. There were numerous young couples he won to Christ over the years who had come to him seeking someone to marry them. He was instant in season and out of season, ready to present the gospel to anyone who came under his influence. People would come to him for counsel with problems. From time to time there would be people in the community calling for someone to help them with their problems. People would come with their marriage troubles or alcohol problems.

Whatever their problem, he tried to help them the best he could, but he always directed the conversation to Jesus and their need to be born again. Over the years, he led many people to Christ in his office as they sought counsel. He was a soul winner. He did the work of an evangelist as ordered by his Commander-in-Chief.

The greater majority of the funerals my father preached were connected with the church. Nevertheless, there always are unsaved people present at funerals. Dad never missed an opportunity to present the gospel at a funeral. Sometimes, that's all a preacher can do. Every minister of the gospel understands the following scenario. He is called upon (perhaps by a funeral director) to officiate a funeral at which he does not know the deceased. Moreover, there is every indication the deceased was unsaved. The pastor knows it, and most everyone else knows the dead man was ungodly. What can he get up and say? To preach the guy into heaven as most liberal preachers do is a violation of scriptural ethics. To stand and denounce the guy as a hell-bound reprobate only brings the anger of many present upon the preacher. Not knowing the fellow makes it very difficult to even eulogize anything good about him. The only recourse is to preach the gospel and reflect how the good of the decedent's death might be someone saved as a result. My father frequently gave invitations at funerals. They may not have been full-fledged altar calls. However, by asking for a show of hands of those who would like to receive Christ and then praying an open prayer asking all willing to silently pray along, Dad saw many come to Christ at funerals. His basic calling was that of a pastor, shepherding the flock the Chief Shepherd had entrusted to him. However, he relentlessly fulfilled the charge of doing the work of an evangelist.

My father lived in one parsonage for over 31 years. It was on the corner of Howard Court and Koch Street in Pekin, Illinois across the street from the church. When we moved into that home in 1958, the house was more or less new, and there were not a lot of homes immediately adjacent. However, as homes began to be built and neighbors began to move in, one by one, my father would witness to them.

One neighbor was Fernie Groth. I think he lived in that house his entire adult life. As early as the late 1950's, Pastor Sorenson sought to witness to him. Fernie would listen and brush him off. He was not particularly interested. But my father kept on witnessing. He kept on praying for his neighbors. If my memory serves me correctly, after at least 20 years, Dad had the privilege of leading Fernie Groth and his wife to Christ. It took a long time. But he just persevered. He never gave up. He kept on praying for them. He kept on witnessing to them. He tried unsuccessfully for more than 20 years to win his neighbor. But one day, the seed sown sprang forth. His faithfulness and persistence in witnessing bore fruit.

Another neighbor moved in across the other corner. She had never been overly interested in the gospel or the church. But little by little he attempted to witness to her. One year she wound up in the hospital. Dad found out about it and through visiting and praying with her was able to lead her to Christ.

Other neighbors built a new house behind the parsonage and moved in. They were not interested in the gospel or the church. But after several decades of being a good neighbor and witnessing to them, Dad was able to lead them to Christ as well.

One thing is for sure. My father was a soul winner. He was not flashy or flamboyant. He just humbly led people to Christ. He won souls. He preached the gospel. He gave invitations to receive Christ every time he preached. He fulfilled the charge given by the apostle to all pastors. He did the work of an evangelist. He obeyed the command issued by the Word of God. He observed what Jesus Christ had commanded him.

To recap, the matter of winning souls is not a gift. It is a command. It is doing the work of an evangelist. God has called some to such a ministry as their full-time calling. However, witnessing and winning people to Christ is a mandate incumbent upon every born-again believer. Of all people, it is mandated for pastors. Once again, the charge given to Pastor Timothy by Paul is set forth in the imperative mode. It therefore is an order. It is a command. And by extension, it is binding upon every pastor since who would be obedient to his high calling.

The Weight of the Great Commission

The last instructions given by Jesus Christ. The command to reach people with the gospel finds even more force when viewed in the greater context of the New Testament. The setting of the Great Commission is most significant. Recall how in each of the several accounts presented between Matthew and Acts, our Lord's commission was issued just prior to his departure from this earth. In regard to His ascension, it is clearest in Acts 1 and Mark 16. It is implied in Matthew 28 as well as Luke 24 and John 20. However, it is indisputable, the several times our Lord gave the Great Commission to His disciples were just prior to His ascension. In other words, it was the last instruction given by Jesus Christ as He ended His earthly ministry.

Though the Great Commission is not a last will and testament in the sense of being issued from one's death bed, there is similar force. Jesus uttered it just prior to His departure for glory. It is the instruction He left for the church in prospect as He departed this world. I will never forget things my father told me the day before he died. They stand out above other things he said over the years. Likewise, the commission of our Lord just before departing this world carry added weight over other things taught throughout His ministry. It was His final word of instruction. It was His last recorded will. He reiterated it several times in His last days on this earth. This adds weight to its priority and importance. The church in general and its leadership in particular have been charged by our Lord to fulfill His commission. It is His parting instruction.

To be sure, there is more to the Great Commission than winning people to Christ. There is the whole spectrum of discipleship as noted in Matthew's account. However, there never will be discipleship unless there is evangelism. Soul winning is the engine which pulls the train of discipleship. Without consistently winning people to Christ, there can be no follow-up or discipling. The latter derives from the former.

Paul's final instruction. In similar fashion, the Apostle Paul issued his charge to Pastor Timothy as he faced his final hours. Immediately after he commanded Timothy to do the work of an evangelist, he said, *"For I am now ready to be offered, and the time of my departure is at hand,"* (II Timothy 4:6). Paul had narrowly missed becoming a spectacle in a Roman arena by being torn to death by lions (II Timothy 4:16-17). But he knew his days were numbered. Indeed they were. Not long after writing his second letter to Timothy, history records he was taken to the edge of Rome, allowed to pray, and then beheaded. When he wrote his second epistle to Timothy, he knew it would be his last. Verses 1-5 of II Timothy 4 form the end of Paul's spiritual charge to Timothy. The remainder of the chapter deals with personal comments about himself and others. Yet, those first five verses contain seven (or eight) imperatives directly related to the pastoral ministry. They in effect form Paul's last will and testament for Timothy. It was the last formal instruction he would give him regarding the ministry. If we take the position the pastoral epistles are by extension in force for New Testament pastors to this day, then the first portion of II Timothy 4 likewise has added weight. Virtually the final thing Paul instructed Timothy as a pastor in his final communiqué was *do the work of an evangelist*! Not only does the charge remain incumbent upon New Testament pastors, it carries the added weight of being essentially the last imperative given by Paul. That leaves this author with the impression, that it is very important. And it is.

One who would seek to be scriptural in fulfilling the pattern of a New Testament pastor therefore must do the work of an evangelist. Do it in your preaching. Do it in personal witness. Be instant in season and out of season. Make full proof of thy ministry. That includes numerous things, but it certainly includes this injunction. It is a part of the solemn and sober charge given by the Apostle beginning in verse 1 of II Timothy 4. It is a part of the string of imperatives issued by Paul for Timothy. By extension, it remains in force for pastors to this day!

Chapter 7 - Take the Oversight Thereof!

"Take heed therefore unto yourselves, and to all the flock over the which the Holy Ghost hath made you overseers."

The **pastor is the overseer**. In an earlier chapter, we dealt at length with the principle how a pastor is enjoined by God to shepherd the flock which God has given him. In I Peter 5:1-2, recall how Peter exhorted elders of local churches to pastor (i.e. shepherd - translated as 'feed') the flock of God among you. We focused on how that involves the love, concern, and spiritual care a pastor ought to have for his people.

However, Peter also enjoined the 'elders' (i.e. pastors) of the church to *take the oversight thereof.* Not only is a pastor to care for his people on an individual basis, but he also is directed to oversee the church collectively. That is, he is enjoined by God to assume oversight which the Chief Shepherd has entrusted to him. **The simple truth is, the pastor is the overseer of the local church**. God has not called any 'church board' or committee to oversee the local church. As noted earlier, the words 'board' or 'committee' as they are commonly used in church polity appear nowhere in the New Testament. Neither does the principle. That is not to say boards or committees are wrong. They certainly have a place. However, there is no mention either by word or precept of such in the New Testament. Interestingly, the word "board" does not appear in the New Testament in regard to deacons. They are called "deacons," never a board of deacons. Check it out.

The pastor is the overseer. Many churches, particularly those of a denominational or associational bent, take the position various boards of the church are the respective overseers. Trustees are elected to oversee church finances. A Christian education committee or board is selected to oversee matters related to Christian education. The deacons are elected presumably to oversee the church spiritually, and so forth. The pastor is the hired preacher who preaches smooth sermons on Sunday, marries, buries, and is the PR man of the church in the community. There is only one thing wrong with such a view. It has no basis whatsoever in the New Testament!

The only individual in the New Testament clearly appointed by God to oversee the local church is the pastor/elder/bishop. (Recall once again how the words "elder" and "bishop" are synonyms for the general title of pastor.)

The word the Holy Spirit inspired Peter to use at this point is of interest. "*Taking the oversight thereof*" is translated from the Greek word "episcopeo." Again, it literally means "to oversee" or "to take oversight." It is formed from two simpler Greek words "epi" which is a preposition having the sense of "over" or "upon." It is coupled to the Greek word "skopeo" which means "to look." Together, the idea literally is "to look over" or "to oversee." That is precisely what God has enjoined the pastor of a local church to do: oversee.

As also noted earlier, the Apostle Paul pled with the elders (i.e. pastors) of the Ephesian church to not only feed the flock of God, but to be diligent in its oversight (Acts 20:28). The word translated "overseers" is "episkopos." It is otherwise translated as "bishop." It is the nominative form of "episkopeo" discussed above. The elder who was charged by Paul to feed the flock (literally "shepherd" as noted in Chapter 2) is also called the overseer of the local church.

Take the Oversight Thereof!

Sadly, many a church board member has been instilled with the idea he has been given charge to oversee the church or some particular portion thereof. Church board or committee members can have an invaluable role in assisting the pastor and the church in providing counsel, advice, and assistance in given areas of church operation. But they are not the overseers! All too often, either through ignorance of New Testament church polity or worse (carnality), pastoral oversight is viewed in terms of power grabbing, "control," or a dictatorship. How many a pastor seeking to discharge his God-given duties has been accused of being a dictator, trying "to control" the church, or being on a power trip? People who think in the terms of, "who has authority, power, and control in a church," reveal either ignorance of Scripture or rebellion against it. The oversight has been given by God to one individual. He most commonly is called the pastor. Like it or lump it. It is the truth! It is scriptural!

God will hold the pastor accountable. The author of Hebrews admonished his readers to *"obey them that have the rule over you,"* (Hebrews 13:17). Lest there be any confusion as to who that is, in verse 7, he wrote, *"remember them which have the rule over you, who have spoken unto you the word of God,"* (Hebrews 13:7). He who speaks the Word of God within the context of the local church is primarily the pastor. However, in verse 17, the scriptural writer went on to note how these *"must give an account."* The one individual in particular whom God will hold accountable for the affairs of a local church is its pastor. If he will be held accountable, then he of necessity must have the prerogative of oversight.

Paul wrote to Timothy the pastor, *"Let no man despise thy youth: but be thou an example of the believer,"* (I Timothy 4:12). Evidently, there were some in Timothy's church who were challenging his leadership based upon his relative youth. Rather, Paul admonished Timothy to not allow that, but be an example of the believer. It is of interest that Timothy was invited by Paul to join him as a young assistant in Acts 16:1-3. It is assumed by many, the events in and about Acts 16 were around A.D. 52. When Paul wrote to Timothy in his first epistle, the time was about A.D. 65. Timothy had been in some form of the ministry for thirteen years. If we assume Paul did not take Timothy as an assistant until he was eighteen years of age, thirteen years later would make him about thirty-one years old. As a thirty-one year old pastor with thirteen years of experience, Timothy nevertheless was admonished by Paul to not allow anyone to diminish or disregard his pastoral leadership, age notwithstanding. God had called and ordained him to pastor. He therefore was urged to not allow anyone to infringe upon his pastoral oversight.

Doctrinal Oversight

Sound doctrine. Let us note five areas of which a pastor has evident scriptural (as well as implied) oversight. Perhaps the most obvious is **doctrinal**. God clearly has given such to a pastor. He is the gatekeeper of what goes forth from the pulpit. This also includes the various extensions of the pulpit in Sunday School teachers or other teachers within the church.

In the three small pastoral epistles (I & II Timothy and Titus), the Apostle Paul refers to doctrine sixteen times. Four of those instances refer to "sound doctrine." Let us take note of each of these passages.

In I Timothy 1:3, Paul admonished Timothy to "*charge some that they teach no other doctrine.*" As pastor of the church at Ephesus, there evidently were some who were deviating in doctrine. Paul charged Timothy to intervene and put a stop to it.

In I Timothy 1:10, Paul described a lengthy list which was contrary to sound doctrine. In I Timothy 4:6, he noted how a good minister of Jesus Christ was one *nourished up in the words of faith and of good doctrine* which Timothy had attained. Later in that same chapter, Paul charged Timothy to among other things "*give attendance . . . to doctrine,*" (I Timothy 4:13). In the final verse of that chapter, he urged Pastor Timothy to "*take heed unto thyself, and unto the doctrine,"* (I Timothy 4:16). In I Timothy 5:17, Paul instructed Timothy how those in pastoral leadership were worthy of double compensation, *"especially they who labour in the word and doctrine."* The apostle also urged Timothy to so teach *"that the name of God and his doctrine be not blasphemed,"* (I Timothy 6:1). Finally, in I Timothy, he warned of those who teach contrary to *"the doctrine which is according to godliness."*

In II Timothy, Paul made four additional comments about doctrine. As his life and ministry were about over, he wrote to Pastor Timothy how he had *"fully known my doctrine,"* (I Timothy 3:10). In the same chapter, he noted how *"All scripture is given by inspiration of God, and is profitable for doctrine,"* (II Timothy 3:16). In the foreboding fourth chapter, Paul charged Pastor Timothy, admonishing him, to *"preach the word . . . with all . . . doctrine,"* (II Timothy 4:2). He warned Timothy how the time was soon coming *"when they will not endure sound doctrine,"* (II Timothy 4:3).

In the small epistle to Pastor Titus, Paul urged him in ordaining "elders" how a "bishop" (notice the two terms are used synonymously) ought *"by sound doctrine both to exhort and to convince the gainsayers,"* (Titus 1:9). In Titus 2:1, Paul directly commanded Pastor Titus to *"speak thou the things which become sound doctrine."* He urged him to show *"himself a pattern of good works: in doctrine,"* (Titus 2:7). Finally, in Titus 2:10, he urged Pastor Titus to so teach his people that *"they may adorn the doctrine of God our Savior in all things."*

As Paul wrote to Pastors Titus and Timothy giving instruction on how to discharge their ministry, it is evident doctrine is a major part. The oversight of doctrine is clearly the purview of the pastor. Someone might protest, what happens when a pastor deviates in doctrine? Though much could be said at this point, there really are only three options. (1) Discuss the matter with the pastor prayerfully, respectfully, and scripturally. If that does not resolve the matter, two options remain: (2) leave the church, or (3) the congregation ask the

The Art of Pastoring

pastor to leave. However, the point to be made at this juncture is the pastor is the God-ordained overseer of doctrine in a local church. That prerogative has never been granted to a committee or board whoever they might be.

Spiritual Oversight

Sense the spiritual temperature of the church and preach accordingly. A second area of pastoral oversight is **spiritual**. By that we mean, God has given to the pastor the responsibility of watching over the spiritual condition of his flock. All manner of spiritual conditions are prevalent in a local church. It is the pastor's responsibility to perceive the spiritual needs of his people and seek to meet them. It may be from the pulpit, the lectern, in home visitation, or counseling in the office. Most of it will come from the pulpit. As noted in an earlier chapter, God's people have spiritual needs ranging from encouragement to conviction over sin. A perceptive pastor will note an individual or family who is sliding back from faithfulness. He will perceive people who need to be encouraged. He will quickly perceive people who are dabbling in sin. God has given each pastor a responsibility to oversee his church and the spiritual condition of his people.

In Acts 20:28, Paul charged the pastoral staff of the Ephesian church to "*take heed therefore unto yourselves, and to all the flock, over which the Holy Ghost hath made you overseers.*" The context clearly is spiritual in nature. Paul went on in the immediate context to warn of wolves entering into the flock from without. Moreover, he warned of those from within who would "*arise, speaking perverse things to draw away disciples after them.*" As Paul defined the qualifications for the office of bishop (i.e. pastor), he noted how a pastor must "*take care of the church of God,*" (I Timothy 3:5). The "taking care of the church" clearly is spiritual in nature. An interesting comment is made by Paul in I Timothy 5:17. There, he is developing the principle of compensation for a pastor. However, in approaching the matter, he speaks of *"the elders that rule well."* The word translated "rule" (proistemi) literally means "to be set before" or "to be set over." A pastor has been "set over" a church. Though the word is translated "rule," the context clearly is spiritual in nature. Note the focus on *"the word and doctrine."*

As Paul urged Timothy to *"follow after righteousness, godliness, faith, love, patience, meekness,"* fighting the good fight of faith, the emphasis clearly is of spiritual oversight. Needless to say, a pastor has been given the prerogative of spiritual oversight of the church. However, with whatever privilege or prerogative there might be, there is a tremendous burden of responsibility. More will be said about that soon.

A wise pastor will seek to perceive where the people are individually. He, however, will also seek to note the spiritual temperature of the church as a whole. Over the years, my father was very sensitive to where the church was spiritually. He frequently would preach against spiritual apathy, indifference, and coldness. On many an occasion, he would warn the people about "grinding out" another service. He always was sensing the spiritual temperature of the church. Then, as he would enter the pulpit, he would seek to stir a spirit of revival in the people. Only as he oversaw the spiritual necessities of the church could he so address its spiritual needs. The pastor is the spiritual overseer of both the collective as well as individual needs of the people.

Organizational Oversight

The pastor is the organizational overseer. The third area of pastoral oversight is **organizational**. In larger churches, pastors at times will appoint an administrative assistant to assist in the organizational operation of the church. That is fine. However, the ultimate oversight still remains with the pastor. I recall a time years ago when I sat as an ex-officio member on a particular church board. I was new as the pastor of the church and attended this particular board meeting for the first time. That board had been delegated oversight of the Sunday School by the church constitution. On some item which I have long forgotten, I made a suggestion. The reply from one of the women on that board was, "This really isn't any of *your* business, pastor!" I was flabbergasted! I had never in decades either in or near the ministry heard a woman in a church tell the pastor matters of the Sunday School were none of his business. About a year later, the church constitution was changed, and that "board" was eliminated along with several others.

New Testament church polity is quite dissimilar from American political structure. Many members in churches carry over the political ideas of American governmental structure and assume it parallels that of the church. New Testament church polity is essentially democratic in nature while American political structure is generally a representative republic. In American civics, the body politic elects representatives who do the business of government. Hence, there are city councils, state legislatures, and the congress respectively. It is often assumed the deacons of a church (or some other board) are elected as representatives of the congregation who are empowered to run the church. However, the deacons (or some other board) were never intended by God to be a "balance of powers" against the pastor. Scripturally, deacons were chosen in the book of Acts to assist the pastor. (They hold a position somewhat similar to that of a wife to her husband. Scripturally, a wife is to be a help-mate for her husband. However, she is to be in submission to her husband.) Both pastor and deacons are accountable to the church, and both can be voted out of office by the church. Scripturally, the church is not a representative republic in its structure. Officers are not elected to "run" the church. God has ordained an overseer for that responsibility. Though accountable to the church, he ultimately is accountable to Jesus Christ. Deacons or other church "boards" ought rather to aid the pastor through assistance and counsel. However, there is no scriptural basis for anyone other than the pastor being the overseer of the church.

The church body elects its officers from the pastor on down. It adopts budgets and policies. It therefore is the responsibility of the pastor to administer the church budget and execute church policy. The deacons of a church are there to assist the pastor in that regard. Scripturally, the pastor is accountable to the congregation, not to the deacons. (However, a wise pastor will certainly give account of himself to his deacons. Over the years, some of my best friends have been my deacons. I covet their counsel, advice, and insight. They truly are help-mates in the ministry, and I love them.) Similarly, whatever authority the pastor may presume has been delegated from the church body and not the deacons (or some board). The simple point is, the pastor in a very practical way remains the overseer, even organizationally.

Administrative Oversight

The pastor is the executive officer of the church. The next (and closely related) area of pastoral oversight is **administrative**. Churches will differ largely in administrative detail based in considerable measure upon their size and adjunct ministries. However, let us present several thoughts philosophically. The pastor is the president of the assembly. He is the moderator of the body in business session. To have someone else assume that position is unscriptural. As the overseer of the church, the pastor is the executive officer. That does not make him the king or the dictator. But he is the God-appointed, church-elected leader.

One of the most rewarding tasks this author has ever undertaken was starting a church "from scratch." Insights into the ministry were gained which many years' experience otherwise did not teach. Things have been learned which could never be learned in college or seminary. In regard to organizational oversight of the local church, a new church is interesting in its philosophical simplicity.

In the early days of the new church, I, as pastor, did everything. At the beginning, I counted the offerings, kept financial records, signed checks, and paid the bills. However, one of the first things done organizationally was to have the young church elect a financial secretary and treasurer. Not only did that free up the pastor, more importantly it took all direct financial dealings from the pastor. In so doing, it fairly well insulated me from any allegations of financial impropriety. I oversaw the Sunday School in its entirety. Eventually, someone was appointed to assume that task. Initially, all records of church membership were kept by myself. However, soon a church clerk was elected. I initially took care of all custodial duties. However, in due season, others were appointed to take care of that task.

I initially heard the testimonies of the first members coming for membership. However, in time, deacons were elected which began to assist in that duty. In the early days, my wife and I personally prepared the elements for the Lord's Supper. Later, deacons and their wives assumed that task. Initially, my wife and I planned all social events of the church. Later, others were appointed to take care of those things. I recall the first youth activities of the church. Guess who organized and directed them? Later, others in the church including an assistant pastor assumed those duties. As the pastor, I typed up the bulletins. Later, others began to assist.

In the earliest days of the church, if it got done, the pastor did it. However, as time passed and the church developed, others began to assume various roles in the ministry of the church. However, the pastor remained the overseer of it all. Long-established churches often forget that at one point a pastor did essentially everything in the church. As time progressed, others were delegated by the pastor or the church to take care of various responsibilities. Unfortunately, some therefore come to think those areas are no longer the pastor's business. However, once upon a time, the pastor did it himself before those duties were delegated to others. That does not abrogate the pastor's prerogative to make organizational adjustments or changes. He still is the overseer of the entire ministry.

Take the Oversight Thereof!

One thing I learned from my father was though others might have been appointed (or elected) to watch over church property and its physical plant, it ultimately came back to the pastor. Until the church was large enough to hire a full-time, salaried custodian, it was the pastor who oversaw the church building. Even when there were staff custodians, there were times when someone forgot to lock a door or turn out lights. Guess who wound up making sure everything was secured and shut down? The pastor did. For years, after each public service, Dad was the last one to leave the building. After everyone else had faded away, he would take a carefully prescribed tour of the entire church plant. He noted every thermostat, every door to make sure it was locked, and every light switch. He stopped in each bathroom to make sure toilets were not running or unflushed. He oversaw the building. The church had several custodians, but they were not always there. The church had a board who in theory was responsible for the church properties. However, none of them ever wanted to hang around to the very end to make sure everything was buttoned up. Dad toured the building every day. Others were assigned tasks such as locking doors and adjusting thermostats. However, people being what they are at times forget, are gone, or overlook some detail. My father caught such organizational oversights. He was the overseer in a very practical way.

I once heard of a pastor who refused to watch over the church building. One winter night, whoever was delegated to turn out lights, turn down thermostats, and lock up was absent. The pastor lived near the church, but he just walked out the door and left the building as it was. He presumably was trying to teach someone to be more responsible. However, the entire church was lit up, heated and unlocked throughout that Sunday night. Rather than bringing reproach upon the party who had failed in his duty, it was the pastor whose stock took a hit because he did not intervene and remedy the situation. The pastor remains the overseer.

I assumed Dad's habit of checking over the building after every service or meeting. Though someone else may have been assigned to lock up, it was common for a youngster to push a panic bar open and not shut the door hard enough to latch. After having witnessed a number of church burglaries and thefts, I came to understand the importance of church security. It falls upon the pastor to either make sure everything was in order or delegate it to a responsible assistant.

Go through channels. My first ministry was as an assistant to Dr. Richard V. Clearwaters. "Doc," as he was affectionately known, was a master of church administration. He noted in a course he taught how most men in the ministry do not fail in the pulpit. Rather, their difficulties arise in church administration. His simple axiom of church administration was "go through channels." Whatever or however a church was organized, wisdom dictated the pastor going through the prescribed channels. Whether the pastor happened to agree with the way the church was organized was beside the point. Until such time an organizational structure could be appropriately changed, there was great wisdom in "going through the prescribed channels."

Frequently, a church has been long in existence prior to the arrival of a new pastor. It may or may not have an altogether scriptural form of church organization. If the pastor is willing to accept a call to the church, he therefore ought to submit himself to its organizational structure. In so doing, he obligates himself to administer the church according to its established structure. That means following the prescribed channels of administration. In time, that organizational structure may be altered. Meanwhile, he should follow the established channels of procedure.

When people have faithfully served the Lord in a church for years in a certain way, they are accustomed to things being done that way. A pastor ought to have the wisdom to defer to that administrative structure until he can wisely persuade the body of the church to do otherwise. Even then, there is great wisdom in making changes slowly. Though the pastor is the overseer, that does not immunize him from dealing foolishly. He ought to have the wisdom to defer to the longevity or grey hair of those who have served the Lord for years in that place.

Financial Oversight

The pastor is the de facto financial controller. A final area of pastoral oversight is **financial**. In most churches, there are elected officers whose duty it is to take care of the actual income and out-go of church funds. Usually, there is someone who is a treasurer who writes the checks and keeps the financial records. Usually, there also is one or several who record individual offering amounts for giving reports and tax purposes. They might be unpaid or staff people. With the exception of a very young church where a pastor may do these chores, it is *very* unwise for a pastor to have any direct contact with church money. It has been said there are three things which get a pastor into trouble: money, morals, and malice. I have known more than one pastor who had to leave a church in disgrace because there were questions over mishandled church funds. The easy solution to that problem is for the pastor to have nothing to do with the actual handling of the money.

My father made it a practice to *not* have his name on any church checking account. He could not write out a check to himself for whatever purpose if he wanted to. He did not count the money. He made it a practice to never look at the offering records. Though as the pastor and executive officer of the church, he certainly could have reviewed them. Nevertheless, he deemed it wise to not know who gave what. He would rather trust the Lord to provide than to rely upon some businessman or benefactor. It gave him much more liberty in preaching. It is surprising to know who tithes and who does not. When a pastor knows someone is heavily lining the church coffers, it becomes difficult to preach about that which might offend him or her. Dad never knew who gave what except as they revealed it to him. His name was not on any church account. He did not go anywhere near where the money actually was.

The Art of Pastoring

Others were the official financial officers. However, my father was the *de facto* financial controller. Though others took care of the day-to-day accounting of monies, he controlled the budget. He watched over it like a hawk on the wing. Prior to going into the ministry, Dad had worked in a bank for ten years. He understood fiscal and budgetary matters. He therefore followed a very simple philosophy of budget management. Always spend less than what you take in. In all the fifty-plus years my father was in the ministry, no church under his leadership ever got into serious financial trouble. To the contrary, in at least one case, he inherited a church which was in financial difficulty and put it back on its feet.

He tracked offering trends weekly and knew exactly how much the church was averaging in its offerings. He then referenced that against the outgo. There are certain things in a church budget which are fixed, the mortgage for example. Other things fluctuate but must be paid such as utility bills. Other things are moral mandates such as being on time in missionary support. However, there are other things which are discretionary. If times were a little tight, he just put the brakes on discretionary spending. On several occasions over the years, he even suspended receiving his paycheck. The ministry came first. There was no way he would allow the church to go into the red under his leadership. Though he did not pay bills himself, he saw to it the church treasurer paid bills promptly and on time. I don't think there ever were times when there were delinquent bills the church owed during his watch. The honor and testimony of the church was at stake, not to mention its credit rating.

When the time came to borrow monies for various projects, there never was any question. The bank knew the track record the church had established under my father's leadership. But by the same token, he was very cautious about borrowing money. Though the church always had good credit, he was extremely conservative about going into debt. However, when the church voted to borrow for whatever, my father saw to it the debt was paid. There were no if, ands, or buts about it.

Take the Oversight Thereof!

Someone has observed, as the personal finances of a pastor go, so go church finances. Pastors usually do not have direct control of church monies. (If they do, they are foolish. They leave themselves wide open to criticism which can destroy their ministry.) Nevertheless, a pastor will exert strong influence over how a church spends. If a pastor personally is a spendthrift, the church he leads will have the same tendency. The alternative is though the pastor may try to lead the church in that direction, deacons or others may drag their feet trying to restrain foolish spending. Friction and trouble inevitably arise. Either the cautious laymen in the church will leave or the pastor will. I have observed more than one occasion where a fiscally undisciplined pastor has caused conservative deacons to leave the church, allowing the pastor to spend as he wishes. However, he quickly wound up paying the piper or at least "owing the piper." I can think of more than one situation where a pastor won a battle over wanting to spend only to find himself in a financial crisis a year or two later. In one case, it was the undoing of his ministry, at least in that church.

Conversely, a pastor who is disciplined and cautious in his personal finances will tend to lead the church in like fashion. My father was certainly of that mold. He left a strong testimony in the business community both in his personal affairs as well as the church's affairs. Moreover, he rarely faced any criticism or questioning from within how monies were handled.

My father took the position that it was the scriptural prerogative of the church to adopt a budget each year. He then, along with the elected officers of the church, administered and executed that budget. He firmly believed he had no authority to spend any more than the church had authorized in its budget. He would not allow shuffling of funds from one account to another to cover a shortfall in a particular area. He believed that bordered upon being deceptive. The truth is, his conservative oversight of church budgets was such, there rarely was a time when a given fund or account could not cover its obligations. His simple administrative philosophy was how neither he nor the other church officers had any right to spend more than what the church had voted to authorize in its budget.

Dad was accountable. He saw to it a detailed financial report of both income and expenditures was presented to the church each month. Every transaction out of the ordinary was always discussed with the appropriate committee or board. He never of his own prerogative authorized anything out of the ordinary without at least conferring with the appropriate church officers. As Dr. Clearwaters always taught, he went through channels. Hence, the financial oversight of the church was usually smooth. On a much more basic level, my father did what was right in this regard. It brought peace in this area of the church for many years.

Technically, the pastor is usually not the official overseer of church finances. Yet, in a very practical way he is. In most situations, the pastor will have a strong influence on how church money is expended. Spending, more than anything else, is what gets a church into financial trouble. When that happens, woe be to the pastor and to the church. Church money troubles bring out the absolute worst in people. More nasty business meetings have been held over unwise handling of church funds than probably any other one thing. Pastors will save themselves ulcers, headaches, and even heart attacks, not to mention much grief, by providing wise, conservative, accountable, disciplined oversight of church spending.

The Burden of Responsibility

The pastor by virtue of his position is in a position of leadership. That has great responsibility. A pastor is the God-ordained overseer of the local church. That involves doctrinal, spiritual, organizational, administrative, and financial oversight. He is not the absolute authority but certainly has the influence of leadership. A wise pastor will seek to lead his church in the paths of righteousness, not only spiritually, but administratively as well. Though he might excel in the pulpit and winning people to Christ, if he is does not properly administer the church, taking the oversight thereof, his ministry will be a rough ride indeed. The simple principle of proper administrative oversight resides in the basic principle of righteousness. Doing right to, for, and by people tends to bring a smooth, peaceful, and happy ministry. Though many a pastor does not set out to be unrighteous, yet by lack of wisdom they accomplish the same. In turn, they find themselves in trouble for what boils down to improper oversight of their church.

With the high office of the pastorate comes a certain degree of privilege, honor, and prerogative. A pastor by virtue of his position is in a place of leadership regardless of the size of the church. However, with whatever privilege of leadership there might be, there is the concomitant burden of responsibility. The whole ministry in one sense rides upon his shoulders. Any man who has been in the pastorate for any length of time understands the concept of carrying the load. In whatever size the ministry, there is a heavy responsibility in being a leader. Even at church social functions when everyone else is relaxed and has their proverbial hair down, the pastor dare not. It really is not a social function for him. It is just another function of the church in which he must set an example and still maintain (perhaps latent, but nevertheless) oversight.

Accountable to Jesus Christ. There is, however, another side of the coin. He is actually an under-shepherd. Though a pastor is the God-called, God-ordained leader of a local church, he actually is representing Another. As a pastor, I am an under-shepherd. The Chief Shepherd is Jesus Christ (I Peter 5:4). The church He has allowed me to shepherd is in reality His flock. It is not mine. It is His which He has *"purchased with his own blood,"* (Acts 20:28). Though I as a pastor certainly am accountable to the church which I serve, I ultimately am accountable to Jesus Christ. Someday, when I stand at the bema, I will be required to give an account to Him.

The author of Hebrews wrote concerning those who quite evidently were pastors in Hebrews 13. In verse 7, he wrote of those *"which have the rule over you, who have spoken unto you the word of God.*" There is little question this refers to the spiritual leadership of the church (i.e., the pastor). Then in verse 17, the text continues to state these same spiritual overseers "*must give account, that they may do it with joy, and not with grief.*" The obvious conclusion is, pastors will some day give an account to the Chief Shepherd. As a pastor, I will someday stand before Jesus Christ not only as my Savior and Lord, but also the One under whom I served. I will in that day give an account to Him how I have fulfilled that responsibility. It is a great privilege to be a pastor, shepherding a local church on behalf of Jesus Christ. However, it is also a great responsibility. I will be held accountable by Him as to how I discharged that stewardship! Moreover, I will someday answer to Him, face to face!

I Peter 5:1-4 clearly indicates for those who have faithfully shepherded their flock, providing proper oversight, there is a coming reward. It is "*a crown of glory that fadeth not away,*" (I Peter 5:4). This author is of the opinion the "*crown of glory*" mentioned is reserved at the bema seat for those who have faithfully and righteously fulfilled a ministry of serving the Chief Shepherd as His under-shepherds. He will in that day duly honor and reward those who have given their lives to so serve Him. Take heart, brother pastor. Though the ministry at times is a battle, and there is a continual load of responsibility, the One whom we serve will richly reward us in that day. It will be worth it all!

Make full proof of thy ministry. Therefore, it is incumbent upon every man who holds the blessed title of "pastor" to faithfully and righteously discharge that calling. In a later chapter, we will look at a number of things which can mar a pastor's ministry. Paul wrote Pastor Timothy to "*make full proof of thy ministry,*" (II Timothy 4:5). The word translated "make full proof" (plerophoreo) essentially means "to fulfill." In other words, the apostle charged us to fulfill our ministry. That in considerable measure involves providing proper oversight of the local church. It is faithfully and righteously overseeing the church in every area. It is incumbent upon every New Testament pastor seeking to scripturally discharge his high calling to provide proper oversight of his church. Anything less is to fail the Chief Shepherd who called and ordained us in the first place. God has given to us not only the privilege but also the responsibility of oversight. Therefore, take the oversight thereof.

I cannot think of another who more righteously discharged the pastoral oversight given to him than my father. He faithfully fulfilled his ministry - to the very end. He made full proof of his ministry. He faithfully discharged the oversight given him by Jesus Christ in pastoring the many years he did.

Chapter 8 - Study to Shew Thyself Approved!

"In his law doth he meditate, day and night."

We are commanded to study God's Word. In his final epistle to Timothy, Paul also charged: *"Study to shew thyself approved unto God, a workman that needeth not to be ashamed, rightly dividing the word of truth,"* (II Timothy 2:15). Like so many of Paul's instructions to Timothy, it was an imperative. As the Holy Spirit inspired him, Paul literally commanded Pastor Timothy to study God's Word. Christians are commanded to study God's Word. Of all people, that applies to pastors.

As a scriptural command, it was not novel. Throughout biblical history, God clearly has commanded His people to study His Word. When Joshua was at the threshold of assuming leadership of Israel upon the death of Moses, God charged him, *"This book of the law shall not depart out of thy mouth; but thou shalt meditate therein day and night, that thou mayest observe to do according to all that is written therein: for then thou shalt make thy way prosperous, and then thou shalt have good success,"* (Joshua 1:8). The construction of the Hebrew text, *"thou shalt meditate therein,"* though technically

The Art of Pastoring

not an imperative, indeed carries the force of an imperative. God, in effect, ordered Joshua to meditate in His Word day and night. As a principle, nothing thereafter in the Bible abrogates that command. It remains in force for God's people to this day.

Even before, God commanded Israel to place His words in their heart (Deuteronomy 6:6). How can someone put God's *words* in their heart without first reading and absorbing them? It begs the idea of study. Not only was Israel commanded to teach God's Word to their children (Deuteronomy 6:7), they were to place plaques of Scripture upon the walls of their homes (6:9). Moreover, they were instructed to *"bind them for a sign upon thine hand, and they shall be as frontlets between thine eyes,"* (6:8). The Pharisees interpreted this literally. They constructed little boxes attached to leather bands in which a small portion of Scripture was written. They then wore those phylacteries, as they were called, like bracelets upon their wrists. Furthermore, they bound phylacteries around their heads such that the little black boxes containing verses of Scripture were upon their foreheads. Sadly, they missed the whole point of what God was teaching His people. In the view of the author, the intent of Deuteronomy 6:8 was spiritual. Binding it upon one's hand and head was a metaphor for having God's Word at hand and on the mind. It, in effect, was a metaphoric way of saying, put God's Word in your heart. However, the Pharisees (along with their modern counterparts, the ultra-orthodox Lubavitchers) have tied God's Word *on* their heads, rather than placing it *in* their hearts. The whole point of Deuteronomy 6 was to so absorb God's Word, teaching it to the coming generation, that they would actually *do* it (6:25). The intent was to read it, memorize it, study it, and absorb it in such a way it changed one's life. It was a command for God's people then. It remains in force as a principle to this day.

In a totally different context, the prophet Isaiah wrote, *"Seek ye out of the book of the Lord, and read,"* (Isaiah 34:16). It is an imperative. It is a command. God ordered His people to check His

Word out. He in effect said, "Go see for yourselves. Read it. Then you will understand!" That imperative remains to this day.

Paul wrote the Colossian church, "*Let the word of Christ dwell in you richly,*" (Colossians 3:16). It is the view of this author, "*the word of Christ*" is the Word of God. Paul in so many words commanded us to cause God's Word to dwell in us. Moreover, he added, "*richly.*" The word so translated (plousios) has the additional sense of "abundantly." In other words, the apostle commanded us to cause God's Word to dwell in us abundantly. That is an elegant way of saying, "study it a lot." It is a command!

In his first epistle to Pastor Timothy, Paul charged him, "*Till I come, give attendance to reading,*" (I Timothy 4:13). Once again, the charge "to read" is an imperative. I would suggest that which Paul admonished Timothy to read was the Word of God. He, in effect, enjoined Timothy in so many words, "Till I come, make a point to read God's Word!" Be attentive to reading it.

Analyzing II Timothy 2:15. Returning to II Timothy 2:15, there is a direct imperative to study God's Word. However, Paul approached it in a way which is not as obvious as the Authorized Version might imply. A literal rendering of the passage might be as follows: "Be diligent to present thyself approved unto God, a workman who needeth not to be ashamed, rightly dividing the Word of truth." Several comments are in order upon this text. The word translated "*study*" (spoudason) has the sense of "diligence." Paul commanded Pastor Timothy to be diligent in presenting (shewing) himself approved by God. How obedience to that injunction is desperately needed to this day! We need be diligent to be found approved by God as we seek to do His work. How few truly seek the potential commendation, "*Well done thou good and faithful servant.*" How we need to seek that same approval. We never will achieve the magnitude of Jesus. Nevertheless, we are enjoined to seek God's approval upon our life and ministry.

Then notice the final qualifying phrase, "*rightly dividing the word of truth.*" It is the key to the whole passage. The word translated "*rightly dividing*" (orthotoumanta) literally means "to cut straight." It was a word used by workmen - e.g., tradesmen who made clean, straight cuts in material. It here was used as a metaphor in regard to the Word of truth. It has the idea of properly understanding it, skillfully applying it, correctly using it, and rightly utilizing it. A craftsman learns to make clean, straight cuts by years of experience. A worker in God's service learns to properly use the Word of God by years of studying it.

Putting it all together, Paul admonished Timothy to diligently seek God's approval upon his work by careful study of His Word. In so many words, he admonished Timothy to be diligent in pleasing God by rightly understanding God's Word and rightly applying it in his ministry. Rightly dividing it, rightly understanding it, rightly applying it, rightly using God's Word comes only by long and careful study thereof. The word "study" used in the Authorized Version accurately summarizes the overall thought to which Paul charged Timothy. We are commanded to so study God's Word that we are pleasing to Him and find ourselves approved by Him. He is the great inspector evaluating our work. It is He who will say (to some, but not all), "*Well done thou good and faithful servant.*" However, His approval will be predicated upon how carefully we have applied His Word to the ministry He has given us.

Hence, it is incumbent upon us to therefore study His Word to such a degree that we are workers approved by God. I would suggest this study be in three ways: devotionally, expositionally, and continually.

A personal student of the Word of God. One of the ironies of life is how a professional in a given field often neglects that professional expertise in his own personal life. I have known more than one mechanic whose own car was unreliable. I know of an accountant whose own personal finances are in disarray. I have met doctors who have had quite unhealthy practices in their lives. Even sadder are pastors who are not personal students of the Word of God. They may understand the Book from their years of formal schooling. They may spend time therein each week developing the various messages necessary for the ministry. Yet, they themselves spend little if any devotional time in the Word.

While in Bible college, it was preached how one of the easiest places to backslide was in a Christian college. The rationale was simple. Young men preparing for the ministry spent much time in formal study of the Scripture to meet requirements for the degree they sought. However, some spent little or no time in day-to-day, personal Bible reading. I fear a similar parallel may exist for men who have been in the ministry for some time. They spend time each week doing the necessary study of the Scripture in preparing sermons and lessons they present. However, their own heart is spiritually barren. It is one thing to study the Bible professionally. It is something entirely different to study God's Word personally.

Study the Word Devotionally

It is therefore crucial for a pastor to study God's Word devotionally. The 37th Psalm develops the juxtaposition between the righteous and the wicked. In verse 31, David wrote concerning the righteous, *"The law of his God is in his heart; none of his steps shall slide."* To place God's Word into one's heart requires an absorption of it to the degree it soaks down from the mind into the heart. Head knowledge rarely changes a life. However, a heart which is saturated with God's Word will be profoundly different from one that is not. The heart is the seat of the will. It is the control center of our decision-making processes. People who often *know better* do evil. The problem is the heart chooses to do wrong. However, a *heart* saturated with God's Word will be profoundly influenced in making decisions and exercising its will. David described a righteous man (verse 30) as having God's Word in his *heart* (verse 31). He went on to note how *"none of his steps shall slide."* Among other things, having a heart saturated with God's Word will bring a stability and balance to life nothing else can.

The Art of Pastoring

Do pastors get into trouble in the ministry? Indeed, they do. It can come in all manner, shapes, and forms. However, I would suggest one of the greatest stabilizing and protective practices a pastor can adopt is spending time in God's Word *personally* and *devotionally* 365 days a year.

Meditating therein day and night. Recall again what God instructed Joshua. Joshua was a soldier, not a preacher. Nevertheless, God ordered him to meditate in His Word *"day and night, that thou mayest observe to do according to all that is written therein: for then shalt thou make thy way prosperous, and then shalt thou have good success,"* (Joshua 1:8). I wonder how many pastors spend time in God's Word *day and night* in a personal and devotional relationship? God promised Joshua as he would so study His Word, he would make his way prosperous. *Then* he would have good success! I am of the view, the promise of God's success and prosperity based upon daily absorption of His Word continues to this day. It is so simple, yet it is so profound. God presented Joshua with a secret for prosperity and success. That principle has never been abrogated.

More than four hundred years later, the Holy Spirit inspired David to comment along the same lines. In Psalm 1, David wrote about the man God would bless. In verse 2, he wrote, *"But his delight is in the law of the LORD; and in his law doth he meditate day and night."* The principle remains unchanged. David continued in verse three, *"whatsoever he doeth shall prosper."* A major secret to finding God's prospering upon our lives is to meditate in His Word, *day and night*.

Let us look a little closer. In both Joshua 1 and Psalm 1, the Holy Spirit used the word "meditate." In both cases, the Hebrew word is "hagah." It has the sense "to study," "to muse," "to imagine," or "to think about." To meditate in His Law is to contemplate His Law. It is to think about it, reflect upon it, or have it upon our mind. No one can think upon the Word of God without reading it. One will not meditate upon it much or for long without reading it. Implicit is the primary concept of first reading. It is then reflecting and thinking about what was read. As God instructed Joshua, the point was to so meditate *"that thou mayest observe to do all that is written therein."* There simply is a linkage between doing what God has written and meditating therein. The idea is the more we meditate in God's Word, the greater influence it will have upon what we do (i.e. how we live).

In both Joshua 1:8 and Psalm 1:2, record is made of meditating *"day and night."* A case could be made how the **maximum** implication of this phrase is unlimited. It is not possible to spend too much time musing upon the Word of God. However, in practice that rarely is the difficulty. To the contrary, most people have problems spending enough time in God's Word. The phrase *"day and night"* is insightful. It likely does not imply spending all our waking hours meditating on God's Word. The word the Holy Spirit used in each case (Joshua 1:8 and Psalm 1:2) for "day" is not the common Hebrew word "yowm," as might be assumed. Rather, it is "yomam," which has the sense of "by day," or "daily." The Hebrew word translated "night" is "layil" and is indeed the common word for night. Together, the phrase has the idea of meditating upon God's Word by day and by night, or daily and by night. In other words, the Scripture teaches one ought to spend time in the Word of God daily and nightly. I wonder how many a pastor actually does that? It would seem the **minimum** implication is how we at the least ought to begin and end the day in the Word of God. Daily and by night would seem to indicate nothing less.

David wrote *"I will meditate in thy precepts"* as well as *"O how love I thy law! It is my meditation all the day,"* (Psalm 119:15,97). Throughout the Psalms, David wrote of meditating in God's Word. He spoke of hiding it in his heart. He wrote of delighting and rejoicing therein. One thing is sure. David, the man after God's own heart, was a man of the Book. He loved it. He studied it. He read it and meditated upon it continually. It so saturated his mind, it soaked down into his heart, modifying not only how he thought, but how he lived. It may be surmised when David eventually did backslide and wallow in the worst of sin, he had drifted out of his long practice of meditating therein day and night.

To so absorb the Word of God has very practical implications. David wrote, "*Thy word have I hid in mine heart, that I might not sin against thee,*" (Psalm 119:11). Saturation of our minds with the Word of God will cause it to soak down into our hearts, thus modifying our decision making processes. The heart is the seat of the will. When the mind has been so saturated with the Word of God it soaks down into the heart, it will influence how we live and the decisions we make. That is what God was driving at when He spoke of meditating "*therein day and night that thou mayest observe to do all that is written therein.*" Meditating in God's Word day and night brings the sufficient quantity to soak in, thus influencing our decisions. Simply put, the more of God's Word we absorb into the heart, the less sin will prevail in our lives.

1. The prevention of sin: Do pastors have a problem with sin? The tragic answer is yes. To be sure, we all have the day-to-day, garden-variety sins of omission and character defects. However, I have known more situations than I care to admit where pastors have had major moral or ethical failures. I have sadly known preachers who have succumbed to adultery. I have known preachers who were involved in less than up-and-up financial dealings. People ask, how could they do that? The answer is simple. At some point, they, like King David, drifted out of God's Word. It no longer was that daily influence soaking down into the heart day and night. They got out of the Word, and the devil snared them. Sadly, legion is the number of pastors in this generation who have washed out of the ministry by some sort of sin in their lives. However, what is more profound but not as obvious is the day they stopped going to the Book on a personal and devotional level. Daily, yea day-and-night, absorption of the Word on a devotional level will prevent sin even in the life of a pastor. Sin is destructive regardless who the party may be. However, <u>when there is sin in the life of a pastor, a whole dark</u>

spectrum emerges. It ranges from the loss of God's blessing and power to the loss of office. God's simple preventative is day-and-night absorption of the Scripture.

2. An example to others: Paul admonished Timothy to be an example of the believer. If there is a basic need people have, it is to be in the Word of God daily. It is difficult for a pastor to exhort his people to go to the Word daily if he himself is not. Not only is it difficult, if a pastor himself is not in the Word, he likely will dodge the issue in the pulpit.

Over the years, I have found simple moral authority in preaching on being in God's Word each day by virtue of a simple fact. I do it daily. I accordingly find it easy to preach on the matter and do with regularity. Though I do not try to set myself forth as a standard before the people, my habit of daily being in the Word of God leaks out in my preaching. They know it. They know I practice it, and therefore it adds credence when I preach upon it.

3. Abiding in Christ: In the great fifteenth chapter of John, Jesus taught the principle of abiding in Him. From so abiding comes all manner of spiritual blessing: fruitfulness, answered prayer, obedience, and discipleship to name a few. However in the view of this author, the quintessence of abiding in Him involves spending time in His Word. Time spent absorbing His Word along with prayer forms the nucleus of abiding in Christ. When a Christian (including a pastor) is not in God's Word on a daily and ongoing basis, it is difficult if not impossible to abide in Him. A pastor not abiding in Christ will find a perfunctory, hollow shell in the ministry. The stream of strength, spiritual power, encouragement, guidance, hope, peace, righteousness, and all manner of spiritual blessings flow from the fountainhead of abiding in Christ who is our life. Practically, that involves time spent absorbing His Word personally and devotionally.

Pastoral burn-out, discouragement, and failure are not uncommon. To be sure, there is always a heavy load in a pastoral ministry. There is an *endless* stream of troubles. There are regular disappointments and let-downs. There are problem people and problem situations. The strength to carry the load and bear the burdens is found by abiding in Him. Yet, the key to abiding in Him is that daily, yea day-and-night, absorption of the Word of God.

One thing which was evident about the life and ministry of my father was His love for the Word of God. He arose early each day to spend time therein. In his study, his Bible was usually open. He revered the Bibles which he owned. His preference was the Thompson Chain Reference Bible. Over his fifty-plus years in the ministry, he only had several copies. As this chapter is being written, there lies upon my desk Dad's Bible. It was purchased decades ago. Many years ago, the binding wore out. Therefore, he sent it somewhere to have it rebound. It came back with a black vinyl kind of cover. It certainly was tougher than the Morocco leather binding from the original publisher. It lasted him the rest of his life. Inside that tough, black, old cover are pages obviously worn and stained with oils of his fingers. Numerous passages are underlined. Numerous notes have been written in the margin. It is an heirloom I will treasure the rest of my days - the blessed Book my father studied, preached from, and wept over for the last half of his ministry.

My father *always* carried a pocket New Testament. It was part of his getting dressed each day. He always had it with him. It was his spiritual weapon from which to witness. It was there to pull out for other spiritual needs. Dad not only hid God's Word in his heart, he carried it on his person - always. He loved the Book of Books. He loved its author. Through it, he abode in Christ throughout his many years of ministry.

Study the Word Expositionally

Study the Book itself. If a pastor would follow the New Testament charge to preach the Word, it is incumbent upon him therefore to study the Book **expositionally** as well. (We might so also describe this as ministerially or professionally.) For a pastor to preach the Word, he must study the Word in such a way as to develop biblical messages. There is absolutely no substitute for a preacher sitting down, digging into the Word of God, using as many helps as necessary, and preparing "from scratch" a message from the Scripture. Anything else is inferior.

I must confess there were times early in my ministry when I obtained a book of sermons by famous preachers and preached what they preached, almost verbatim. I reasoned, if they preached such messages with great results, maybe I could as well. I suppose every preacher has been guilty of such. I am not critical of books of sermons as a source of ideas and illustrations. However, the basic source book for a biblical message must be the Word of God. Years ago, I purchased a set of books containing the best sermons of Spurgeon. As I was starting out preaching, I would take one his sermons, rework it a bit, and then preach it myself. The only problem was, I was preaching Spurgeon and not the Word. I am no Spurgeon. I could not begin to approach the level of eloquence and depth he had. To try and use his sermons is tantamount to you or me trying to drive the lane like Michael Jordan. Only he can do it the way he does. Moreover, Spurgeon preached to a different era (Victorian England) which had a different level of vocabulary, and lived in a totally different culture. I value Spurgeon, but for me to use his sermons is naive.

I have known preachers down through the years who wait until Saturday night to prepare a message for Sunday morning. Apart from the obvious lack of self-discipline and organization, waiting until Saturday night to prepare a message is giving short shrift to not only the congregation on Sunday morning, but to the Chief Shepherd as well. Adequate preparation becomes almost impossible on such short order.

My father always had his messages ready to go several days, if not a week or two in advance. He sat down with an open Bible, spent time in prayer asking the Holy Spirit to give the seed-thought of

The Art of Pastoring

direction, and then went to the Word to develop the message. His messages were always biblically based and biblically studied.

I once knew a pastor who would often wait until Saturday night to try and come up with a message for Sunday morning. He would even call another preacher friend at 10 o' clock that night and ask him for sermon ideas. I have no idea how such message preparation played out on Sunday morning. However, I know he eventually washed out of the pastoral ministry.

Go to the book. I am amazed at the various and sundry sermon services which are advertised across the land. In some cases, I suspect they are geared for liberal preachers who have run out of anything to say. In other cases, they are geared for evangelical pastors who are too busy doing other things than preparing messages for the pulpit on Sunday morning (not to mention for Sunday evening, Wednesday night, and Sunday School). I have further seen sermons offered on a weekly basis designed for fundamental pastors. Such an advertisement from a proclaimed fundamentalist preacher crossed my desk the week this chapter was being written. How can a pastor claim he is preaching the Word when in fact his sermon came in the mail? Maybe the sermon service offered good material. However, it never can be a substitute for gleaning a message directly from the Book of Books with the help of the Holy Spirit for the needs of the congregation present. Only the pastor of a local church with the assistance of God's Spirit knows what a church needs spiritually from week to week.

Getting sermons from a book or a sermon service is like putting a TV dinner on the table each Sunday. In a pinch, it will get by. However, a steady diet of such will grow old fast. On occasion, I confess I have gone to the filing cabinet, pulled out a message I preached years ago, and delivered it on Sunday. However, there usually were mitigating circumstances involved necessitating such a device. When the church was in a building program, and I as pastor was involved in supervision on a daily basis, I resorted to such message preparation more than once. But it was extraordinary circumstances. I was, in effect, was delivering "left-overs" from the pulpit. I tried to cover the staleness, but I am sure those in the pew detected it. If such message preparation continued over the long run, I am sure I would have been looking for another place.

Preparing a sermon is not unlike preparing a meal. How can one preach the Word if he does not study the Word? As most long-time preachers know, message preparation involves more than devotional study. There must be an understanding of what the Scripture says. It must be placed upon the kitchen counter of a pastor's desk and prepared into a form which is both palatable and spiritually nutritious to the ears for which it is intended. It involves placing it into the oven of prayer and cooking it with the oil of the Holy Spirit until the message is done and ready to be served from the pulpit.

There are all manner of types of sermons. Some are intended to evangelize. Others are intended to edify, others to encourage, others to convict, others to instruct, still others to motivate. There are several different formats such as topical, textual or expositional. But whatever the purpose or format, proper preparation is the same. It is studying the Word of God to such a degree a message from God is absorbed by the preacher's study. Most fundamental pastors will deliver as many as two hundred *different* messages a year. That is preaching on Sunday morning and evening as well as a midweek message and a Sunday School lesson each week. Fortunately, the Word of God is an infinite source of preaching material. There is no bottom to the well of God's Word. All a preacher needs to do is study it. It is work. It is time-consuming. It requires self-discipline. And, it is most helpful to be conversant with the various tools useful in studying and preparing messages.

Bible Colleges and seminaries exist to train young men in the tools of studying God's Word for message preparation. In recent years, computerized Bible study programs have become common. They are a great time-saving device in message preparation for busy pastors. They are comparable to power tools for a carpenter.

Nevertheless, even with power tools available, message preparation is work and requires time. A pastor must study God's word ministerially. There are no shortcuts. There are no quick fixes. To preach the Word means studying the Word. It requires time, work, prayer, reliance upon the Holy Spirit, and the self-discipline to sit down and do it.

Henry Sorenson studied for every message he delivered. Virtually every morning of the work-week, he was in his study. On his desk was an open Bible. Beside it was whatever other books and helps he used in preparing upcoming messages. He dug into the Word. He studied daily. He followed that general procedure for more than fifty years. Then, after having prepared the various messages and lessons which he presented each week, he went back late in the week and did further review and preparation. On Saturday mornings, he was in his office early, going over what he was going to preach the next day. On Saturday evening, he was back in his study once again reviewing and "prepping" for message delivery on the Lord's day. Then early on Sunday morning, he was in the study again for final review, prayer, and message polishing. He did the same late in the afternoon on Sunday in preparation for the evening service. He studied to show himself approved unto God. It showed in the pulpit each week.

Study the Word Continually

Giving attendance to reading. As noted earlier, a pastor needs to study God's Word, *devotionally* and *ministerially*. However, let us suggest a third way. A godly pastor needs to study God's Word **continually**. James wrote, *"But whoso looketh into the perfect law of liberty, and continueth therein, he being not a forgetful hearer, but a doer of the work, this man shall be blessed in his deed,"* (James 1:25). I once heard a Christian leader for whom I had respect make the comment how in the early years of his ministry, he spent time every morning studying God's Word both devotionally and for message preparation. In his later years in the ministry, his ministry was such that he was not a pastor preparing fresh messages three or four times a week. Though he did not say so in so many words, he implied he no longer spent the time each day he once did in studying God's Word. I thought it strange how a spiritual leader would publicly admit he didn't study the Scripture as much as he used to do.

Never stop studying. Notwithstanding that man's practice, it is the view of this author how God has admonished (of all people) those in spiritual leadership to study His Word continually. The Holy Spirit inspired James to use the word "parameno" which is translated "continueth" in the Authorized Version. It literally means "to remain beside" or "to continue always." If I understand that right, God in His Word has instructed us to *continue always* in His Word. We will never outgrow the Scripture. The injunction to meditate therein day and night is not lifted after so many years. In some areas of government service or private business, an individual after working for 30 years can retire with full benefits. However, there is nothing to indicate that is the case in God's work. Certainly, it is not the case concerning God's Word.

Even in retirement, my father carried his pocket New Testament. It was always ready to be used in witnessing. On his desk, even in retirement, was his Bible. It usually was open as when he was full-time in the pastorate. He never quit. He studied to show himself approved unto God even after he no longer had a regular pulpit to fill. He continued therein.

Seven times a year? Years ago, I heard a preacher stand and speak to the matter of reading God's Word through, cover to cover, seven times a year. I was well aware how God charged Joshua to meditate therein day and night, as well as David's comments concerning the same. I reasoned, if he can read the book through seven times a year, so can I. I am no busier than he, probably even less. I came home from that conference determined to embark upon a schedule of reading the Word of God through seven times in the coming twelve months. The initial enthusiasm quickly faded. After

The Art of Pastoring

several days, it was evident reading that quantity of Scripture daily would be a task. I was tempted to give up on the idea. However, I determined to forge ahead and accomplish the goal for at least one year. That was about 24 years ago. The way I approach the challenge has changed some over the last two decades, but the basic goal remains the same.

Few things, in my opinion, have had a greater influence upon my ministry than reading the Word of God through seven times each year. It without a question has given me a basic framework from which to spend time in God's Word day and night. Without this goal, I know I would not spend as much time studying the Scripture. It has given me an ongoing overview of the Scripture. To be sure, it is not in-depth study. Rather, it is a continual refreshing of the overall themes of God's Word. The practice continually gives insight into overall context and content. That overview therefore has greatly added insight into understanding a given passage and its relation to the whole of Scripture. It has truly caused God's Word to soak down into my heart and has profoundly influenced my life. As long as health prevails and the Lord tarries His coming, I intend to continue therein the remainder of my days. It truly has been one of the great blessings of my Christian life.

One might enquire about the mechanics of reading the Scripture through seven times a year. I long ago determined to read 27 chapters a day Monday through Thursday which is the bulk of my work-week and 18 chapters a day Friday through Sunday which is the essence of my weekend. That gives a cumulative total of reading the Book through seven times a year with some to spare for sick days or times of unusual schedule. (I often read more on the weekends than prescribed to account for times I might miss during the week.) I have generally broken my reading schedule into three times a day in which I read nine chapters each. That generally is the (1) first thing in the morning when I rise, (2) over the noon hour, and then (3) sometime during the evening prior to bedtime. It has become a habit which has kept me in God's Word literally day and night for almost a quarter of a century.

In the early years of such reading, I tried to read from each section of the Bible daily. Therefore, I read five chapters a day from the Pentateuch, four chapters day from the history books, three a day from the poetry books, four from the major prophets, two from the minor prophets, three from the gospels, one from either Acts or Revelation, three a day from the Pauline Epistles and two from the general epistles. That totals 27. It kept me in each section of the Scripture daily. Later, I went to simply reading straight through the Bible book-by-book to maintain contextual continuity. However, the 27 chapters a day remained the same. Either way, I was in God's Word day and night every day. It has truly revolutionized my understanding of God's Word. And, it has been one of the great blessings of my life.

The greater principle is to study God's Word to such a degree we are workmen approved unto God, rightly dividing the Word of truth. That involves studying it devotionally, ministerially, and continually. It will be a great key to God's blessing upon the life and ministry of any pastor.

Chapter 9 - Pray without Ceasing!

"I exhort therefore, that, first of all, supplications, prayers, intercessions, and giving of thanks be made for all men."

Prayer is the unseen ingredient. We come to the invisible part of a pastoral ministry. Preaching, working with the people, overseeing the ministry of the church, and doing the work of an evangelist are noticeable. However, one of the most important elements in a pastoral ministry is not, at least as it is accomplished. Prayer is something of which only God is totally aware. It is the invisible part of being a pastor, yet it is crucial. Success or failure in the pastoral ministry probably has more to do with the time spent alone with God in prayer than any other one thing.

As I look back over the ministry of my father, if there is one thing which characterized him, it was prayer. He was a prayer warrior. Dad was not the most eloquent preacher in the world. But he built a great church. He was not known for charisma or magnetism in his personality. To say he was of humble and lowly estate would be an accurate statement. However, Henry Sorenson was well known before the throne of grace. He was a long and frequent visitor thereto. At his funeral, about a dozen preachers stood and gave testimony of his ministry. One thing which stood out was how he was a man of prayer. Over the years, there were many times I came into the church and found my father on his knees before a pew. There were numerous times I knocked on his study door only to realize I had interrupted him in prayer. It was the secret of his ministry. Dad was not a master of marketing or promotion, but he knew how to pray. With several short exceptions, he never had a radio broadcast (much less a television program). But he knew how to transmit to the Chief Shepherd. He never authored any books, but he was intimate with the Author of authors. He knew how to pray.

The imperative of prayer. As we have developed a number of imperatives pertaining to the pastoral ministry, let us consider another. In the latter portion of I Timothy 1 and into Chapter 2, the Apostle commanded Pastor Timothy to pray. From verse 18 flows the admonitions and injunctions of Chapter 2. Paul wrote, *"This charge I commit unto thee, son Timothy, according to the prophecies which went before on thee, that thou by them mightest war a good warfare,"* (I Timothy 1:18). The word translated "charge" (paranggelia) has the sense of a command and is so translated elsewhere. In essence, Paul wrote to Timothy how he was giving him a commandment. He noted further how this charge (commandment) was *"according to the prophecies which went before on thee."* Indeed, it is the Scripture which will enable us to *"war a good warfare."*

However, I Timothy 2:1 is where this first command begins. There, Paul wrote, *"I exhort therefore, that, first of all, supplications, prayers, intercessions, and giving of thanks be made for all men."* Therefore, as the *first* epistle to Timothy unfolds, the *first* command issued is to pray! That is to what the *"first of all"* alludes. It was Paul's *first* major instruction to Pastor Timothy. Though other elements of the ministry are seen in their doing, prayer is the invisible element. Nevertheless, it may be the most important.

Paul commanded Timothy *"first of all"* to pray. It is the secret to God's power, blessing, and strength.

The apostle noted five areas of prayer. Though some may seem redundant, there are nuances of distinction nevertheless. Let us look more closely.

Supplications

Prayer is asking. The first is (1) "**supplications**." It is translated from the word "deesis" and has the sense of making petition. In more common terms, it means to ask or to seek. In regard to prayer, it has the idea of asking God for needs or making requests. It can apply both for our own requests or on behalf of another. The idea is richly illustrated throughout the Bible. For example, Jesus taught his disciples: *"Ask, and it shall be given you; seek, and ye shall find, knock, and it shall be opened,"* (Luke 11:9). James wrote how *"Ye have not because ye ask not,"* (James 4:3). Most cases of fervent prayer in the Bible revolve around someone begging God to do something. It may have been Jehoshaphat begging God to deliver Judah from the Assyrians in II Chronicles 20:12. It may have been Hannah pleading with God to give her children in I Samuel 2. It may have been Daniel pleading with God to show mercy to Israel. Jesus besought His heavenly Father to take the cup He was about to drink from Him, yet surrendering to His will. To supplicate is to make request. It is to ask. It is to petition. The term itself is neutral whether request is for ourselves or others.

A veteran pastor knows there is no end to prayer needs in the ministry. It may be for himself asking God for spiritual power, wisdom, strength, guidance, provision, or numerous other things. It may be asking God to help, bless, or meet the needs of people, missionaries, or other worthy matters. The first command for Timothy's pastoral ministry was to pray. Specifically, it was to make request to God for the needs and problems of which the ministry is surrounded.

The Art of Pastoring

Few people see the pastor's prayer closet, but it is where He meets with God. It may be in his study beside his desk. It may be in his bedroom beside his bed. It may be in his car as he drives down the road. It may be in the church auditorium when it is empty. It may be in the woods where he resorts to the cathedral of the pines to meet with God. It may be along the beach or beside a body of water. But it is time alone with God making request for the numerous needs in and around his ministry.

Prayers

Prayer involves praise and worship. Paul then continued with a word which in English may seem repetitious. Yet, upon closer examination, a whole new spectrum of thought is revealed. He commanded Timothy that (2) "**prayers**" be made. Though the thought may seem redundant, the word Paul chose has a different nuance. That word, "proseuche," has the literal sense of "prayer addressed to God." The idea is of approaching God in worship and praise. Without question, there is more to praying than just asking. Much communication to God on our part ought to be praise. For example, the "hallel" Psalms - those beginning or ending with "*Praise ye the LORD*" - are largely prayers uttered by David. It is clear - David was serious about praising the Lord. In the view of this author, a major aspect of praise ought to be found in one's prayer life. Moreover, this author takes the position how the most basic form of worship takes place in prayer. It is there we can praise God multiple times daily. David wrote, "*Seven times a day do I praise thee because of thy righteous judgments,*" (Psalm 119:164). That likely refers to prayer. As Jesus presented what traditionally is called the Lord's Prayer, He began by instructing His disciples to pray, "*Our Father which art in heaven, hallowed be thy name,*" (Matthew 6:9). The word translated "hallowed" is "hagiadzo" which literally means "to sanctify" or "to make holy." (Actually, the phrase has the sense, "holy is thy name.") In so doing, Jesus said, when you pray, begin by praising God. Though called the Lord's Prayer, it actually was a lesson in which Jesus taught his disciples how to pray through the example He set forth. More accurately, it could be called a pattern prayer. The greater point is how we ought to praise and worship God as we pray. That is the implicit sense contained in the word "proseuche," translated "prayer" in I Timothy 2:1.

Intercessions

Prayer is fellowship with God. The next word is (3) "**intercessions**." In modern vernacular, the assumption is of interceding on behalf of another. That is a derived sense. However, it does not convey the core idea. The end of the verse at hand clearly refers to interceding for others, but there is a more profound idea at hand. The word in question is "enteuxis." Its most basic sense is "to meet together with another." It has the idea of conversation or communion between two. The greater idea is communion with God. It is our spirit in communion with Him. It implies spiritual intimacy, communication, and fellowship. It is what Enoch did when he walked with God in Genesis 5. It, by implication, is what Adam, Eve and God did prior to the fall. It is personal fellowship.

Pardon an illustration from my personal life. My wife and I do not see each other much during the day. Though we may talk briefly on the phone, in the evening, we sit down and talk about what went on that day. It usually is small talk of no great consequence. But we have fellowship and communion one with another. And so it ought to be with God. Though we may come to Him in praise worshiping Him; and though we may make requests before Him, He also desires us to simply commune with Him.

The thought implied bespeaks conversation, a conference, or a coming together. As the one once said, "And He walks with me and He talks with me, and He tells me I am His own. And the joy we share as we tarry there, none other has ever known."

Giving of thanks

Prayer includes giving of thanks. Paul charged Pastor Timothy that (4) *"giving of thanks be made."* The principle of thanksgiving abounds throughout the Bible. By one count, there are more than one-hundred-thirty references to thanks in the Scripture. The vast majority pertain to thanking God. It ought to be a part of our daily prayer life. There are innumerable things for which we should be thankful. Therefore, each day, as we go to prayer, we ought to give thanks. It ought be an integral part of one's prayer life.

For all men

Prayer should be for others. Finally, Paul went on to note how in praying, we ought to do so (5) *"for all men."* Particularly, making requests ought to be for others and their needs. This is the matter of intercession. Of all people, a pastor ought to be a master of intercessory prayer. He has an entire congregation for which to pray. The needs of his people are almost unlimited. There are spiritual needs, health needs, financial needs, not to mention emotional needs. As a pastor, there is no end in praying for my people. Their needs vary, but one thing never changes. <u>They need someone to pray for them.</u> Our Lord has set the example for us. Even as we speak, He is interceding for us at the right hand of God. Therefore, we as pastors ought also to intercede for our people.

When I was a teenage boy, we lived across the street from the church. I would from time to time go across the street to look up my father for whatever. I walked through the old auditorium of the church towards his study. On more than one occasion, there was Dad on his knees at the front row. Before him was a copy of the church membership roll. He was systematically praying for the people of his congregation. It was the quintessence of intercessory prayer.

The apostle charged Timothy to pray not only for all men (i.e. everyday people), but also *"for kings, and all that are in authority."*

Pray without Ceasing!

We are commanded to pray for those in leadership. The greater thrust is how a pastor ought to pray. In fact, Paul charged Pastor Timothy *"first of all"* to pray, making requests for whatever needs are at hand.

Pray, praising and worshiping God. Pray, having simple communion with Him. Pray, thanking Him for His manifold blessings. Finally, pray for others and their needs. This charge remains incumbent upon all who hold the title of pastor.

The truth is, God has commanded all Christians to pray. Therefore, how much more ought a pastor to pray. Luke records how Jesus taught His disciples, *"Men ought always to pray, and not to faint,"* (Luke 18:1). The thrust clearly is a command. God's people ought always to be praying and not giving up though God *"bears long with them"* (Luke 18:7). Yet, the more obvious principle is to just keep on praying. If the person in the pew is so enjoined, how much more the pastor?

Praying Always

Pray continually. Paul wrote the Roman church about *"continuing instant in prayer,"* (Romans 12:12). The word translated "continuing instant" (proskartereo) has the idea "to continue," "to be steadfast," "to persevere," or "to not quit." The injunction is simple. Keep on praying. Now if that is true for the average Christian in everyday living, how much more is it true for the one who is the leader of the church?

The apostle wrote the Ephesian church to be *"praying always,"* (Ephesians 6:18). That is the capstone of his charge to *"be strong in the Lord,"* putting on the whole armor of God. The strength for the battle comes as we spend time in the presence of Him who is strength. David knew that. He cried out a thousand years earlier, *"The LORD is the strength of my life,"* (Psalm 27:1). One might have the whole of armor of God upon him, yet not have the strength to continue. *Praying always* girds the strength needed to join the battle.

The phrase translated *"praying always"* could literally be translated "praying in all times," or "praying all the time."

That is what Paul wrote in I Thessalonians 5:17, *"Pray without ceasing."* Again, it is an imperative. The word translated "without ceasing" (adialeiptos) has the idea "without intermission, continually, or incessantly." The Scripture clearly builds a case how we ought always be in a state of prayer. When I wake up in the middle of the night and cannot sleep, I begin to pray. As I walk the lane to the mail box each day, I often pray. As I drive around town, I turn off the radio and pray. As I regularly go for an aerobic walk, I pray. If I am traveling alone on long distance trips, it is a wonderful time to pray. Though we cannot readily be in the Word as we go about all the day-to-day routines of life, we can have our heart transmitting on heaven's frequency. It is a wonderful way to stay in touch with headquarters on a regular basis.

Prayer is an antidote to temptation. Incidentally, we touch upon a major way of precluding sin in our lives. Jesus said, *"Pray that ye enter not into temptation,"* (Luke 22:40). When my mind is dialed to heaven's number and I am communicating with the Strength of my life, Satan cannot get through. The line is busy. Prayer will shut out the world, the flesh, and the devil. It is an effective side-benefit to an otherwise wonderful spiritual experience. Pastors get into trouble because either (1) they are not in the Word day and night, or (2) they are not continually in prayer. God's way is simple.

In that same vein, Paul wrote to the church at Colosse, *"Continue in prayer,"* (Colossians 4:2). He used the same basic word as he did in Romans 12:12. It is set forth in the imperative mode; it is a command; it is an order. Once again, if the church in general is commanded to pray, how much more its leadership? The collective command of the New Testament in this regard is for God's people to be in prayer all the time. Of all people, that again applies to pastors.

The Example of Jesus

To be like Jesus is to pray continually. If we would be conformed to the image of His Son, it is incumbent upon us to pray. Our Lord's earthly ministry was characterized by personal prayer. For example, notice Matthew 14:23. *"And when he had sent the multitudes away, he went up into a mountain apart to pray: and when the evening was come, he was there alone."* Jesus went out of His way to find places suitable for prayer alone with God. Mark records the same situation in Mark 6:46.

On another occasion, Mark wrote, *"And in the morning, rising up a great while before day, he went out, and departed into a solitary place, and there prayed,"* (Mark 1:35). If the time were near the winter solstice, the hour may not have been as early if it were near the summer solstice. However, that is beside the point. Jesus got up early in the morning, went out, and found a place of solitude to pray. Though not otherwise noted, it might be surmised that Jesus made it a practice to begin the day in prayer.

As Jesus officially began His earthly ministry, He chose His twelve disciples. It obviously was a significant event. In that context, notice how the preceding night, *"he went out into a mountain to pray, and continued all night in prayer to God,"* (Luke 6:12). In His omniscience, Jesus very well knew who His disciples would be. However, His prayer during the night may have been asking God to so work in their hearts, they would answer His call. In any event, He spent the entire night in prayer prior to a major event in His ministry.

At another time, Luke wrote how, *"it came to pass, as he was alone praying, his disciples were with him,"* (Luke 9:18). The occasion was His inquiry, *"Whom say the people that I am?"* The point however was Jesus again alone in prayer.

Shortly thereafter, *"He took Peter and John and James, and went up into a mountain to pray,"* (Luke 9:28). Before His transfiguration, Jesus got alone to pray.

Luke later notes *"as he was praying in a certain place . . . one of his disciples said unto him, Lord teach us to pray,"* (Luke 11:1). His disciples noticed His frequent prayer time and asked Him to teach them how to so pray. On another occasion, Luke wrote, *"He withdrew himself into the wilderness, and prayed,"* (Luke 5:16).

Each of the synoptic gospels records Jesus' season of impassioned prayer at Gethsemane. As He approached the ultimate crisis of His ministry, He could only fall on His face before God and pray. Mark wrote, *"And they came to a place which was named Gethsemane: and he saith to his disciples, Sit ye here, while I shall pray"* (Mark 14:32). Then in verse 35 we read, *"And he went forward a little, and fell on the ground, and prayed."*

One thing is sure. Jesus was a man of prayer! At every juncture in His ministry, He prayed. He prayed early in the day. He prayed late in the day. He prayed in solitude. He prayed with His disciples. Jesus indeed left an example that we should follow in his steps. If we as under-shepherds would be like the Chief Shepherd, it is incumbent upon us to pray as He prayed.

The Example of Paul

Paul's ministry was characterized by endless prayer. On several occasions, Paul wrote, *"Be ye followers of me, even as I also am of Christ,"* (e.g., I Corinthians 11:1). What he was driving at was for God's people to follow his example. In regard to prayer, Paul set forth an extensive standard. He practiced what he preached. He wrote the Ephesian church, *"Wherefore I also, after I heard of your faith in the Lord Jesus, and love unto all the saints, cease not to give thanks for you, making mention of you in my prayers,"* (Ephesians 1:15-16). He then proceeded to embellish on how he prayed for them. In similar fashion, he described further prayer for them in Ephesians 3:14. *"For this cause I bow my knees unto the Father of our Lord Jesus Christ."* He mentioned even more of his prayer in the succeeding verses.

In writing to the Colossian church, Paul wrote, *"For this cause we also, since the day we heard it, do not cease to pray for you,"* (Colossians 1:9). As in his Ephesian epistle, he went on and detailed how he prayed for them. (It is not our purview to examine the content of Paul's prayers as he made note of them. However, there is a profound depth of spiritual character and concern. This indeed is insightful from the one who has encouraged us to be a follower of him.)

He wrote the Thessalonian church he was *"night and day praying exceedingly that we might see your face, and might perfect that which is lacking in your faith,"* (I Thessalonians 3:10). When he wrote them again, he mentioned, *"Wherefore also we pray always for you,"* (II Thessalonians 1:11). One thing is evident. As a spiritual leader, Paul set a high standard for us in his prayer life. He mentioned how he prayed night and day. He prayed for needs from the day he became aware of them. He wrote about how he did not cease to pray for others. As the Holy Spirit inspired him, he wrote, *"Be ye followers of me even as I also am of Christ."* There are many aspects of Paul's ministry afer which we might pattern our ministries. However, one is his prayer life.

The Pastor's Prayer Life

Let us consider a number of areas around which a pastor ought to frame his prayer life.

1. Fellowship with Christ - More than anything else, a pastor needs to be in fellowship with the Savior. Jesus said, *"Abide in me, and I in you. As the branch cannot bear fruit of itself, except it abide in the vine; no more can ye, except ye abide in me,"* (John 15:4). The word translated "abide" (meno) simply means to "dwell," or to "remain." It also has the sense "to continue" or "to tarry." To abide in Christ is to remain with Him. It is to tarry together with Him. That certainly involves time in His Word. But it also clearly involves time in prayer. It is good to have fellowship with my wife. It is good to

The Art of Pastoring

have fellowship with other brethren. But it is crucial to have fellowship with Christ. Though we cannot always be in the Word, we can always be in a spirit of prayer. It is the spiritual cell-phone which keeps us in touch with the Chief Shepherd. We can pray as we drive. We can pray as we sit at the desk preparing a message. We can pray before or during virtually any activity.

A fascinating example of being instant in prayer is found in the life of Nehemiah. Upon learning of the devastation at Jerusalem, Nehemiah determined to approach his lord, King Artaxerxes of the Persian empire. His objective was to obtain permission to go to Jerusalem and rebuild its wall. He was the cup-bearer of the king and hence on familiar terms with him. As he approached the king, Artaxerxes asked him, *"For what dost thou make request? So I prayed to the God of heaven. And I said unto the king . . .,"* (Nehemiah 2:4-5). What is interesting is how Nehemiah breathed a prayer for help in the middle of his conversation before the king of the Persian empire. He evidently was in such fellowship with God, he felt no reluctance to pray on the spot, even under his breath. What is further implied is how Nehemiah was otherwise on quite familiar terms with God. He obviously spent much time in prayer with Him. Though in an Old Testament context, he abode in Christ.

Before a pastor seeks fellowship with any other, he ought first become a regular "client" at the throne of grace. Though the Lord in His omniscience certainly knows us, there ought to be an intimacy of long standing fellowship which causes Him to know us on a personal basis. That comes only by spending much time in prayer with Him. To abide in Christ is to be in regular fellowship with Him. It is being in constant touch with Him through prayer. It is continuing with Him. It is tarrying with Him. That personal fellowship of spiritual intimacy becomes the foundation from which all other "ministerial prayer" derives. Nehemiah evidently had a close fellowship with the Lord and could whisper a prayer in the midst of a crucial conversation. So ought our spiritual intimacy to be with our Lord and Savior.

2. Power with God - A pastor needs the power of God in His ministry. That spiritual power manifests itself in the conviction by the Holy Spirit. It is true whether the gospel is issued from the pulpit or in one-to-one personal soul winning. However, the power of God is a result of the filling of the Holy Spirit. In tracking the fullness of the Spirit through the Word of God, it is evident one crucial element always present is prayer.

For example, the apostles and the early church had spent what amounted to a ten-day prayer meeting between Acts 1:14 and Acts 2:1. However, as the day of Pentecost was fully come, *"they were all filled with the Holy Ghost,"* (Acts 2:4). That day, as Peter preached and the eleven witnessed, three thousand souls were saved. The power of God manifested was a result of the filling of the Holy Spirit upon Peter and the eleven. However, what is less obvious is how they had spent days in prayer prior thereto. Notice also in Acts 4:24 where the early church facing stiff persecution had gone to prayer. The following text notes, *"And when they had prayed, the place was shaken where they were assembled together; and they were all filled with the Holy Ghost, and they spake the word of God with boldness . . . and with great power gave the apostles witness of the resurrection of the Lord Jesus,"* (Acts 4:31,33). Notice the sequence. Their great power in witnessing was predicated upon being filled with the Holy Ghost. However, the fullness of the Holy Spirit was predicated upon fervent prayer on behalf of the church and its leadership. In most places in the Scripture where the power of God is present, it was directly linked to the moving of the Holy Spirit (i.e., the filling of the Spirit). However, usually in the background, though not as obvious, was extensive prayer.

A pastor, therefore, ought to spend significant time in prayer to be filled with the Holy Spirit. If he would have the power of God upon him as he enters the pulpit, somebody surely will have been praying. The story has been told repeatedly of an incident in Spurgeon's ministry. A visitor inquired of the source of his great power in preaching. Since it was near the time of a service, Spurgeon took him aside to a room. He opened the door, and there were people on their knees praying. Spurgeon reportedly informed his guest how he never entered the pulpit without people praying for him. However many people a pastor might have praying for him as he preaches, he himself must spend time in prayer seeking the fullness of the Holy Spirit. It is vital and essential.

3. **Guidance** - If there is anyone who needs guidance along the path of the Christian life, it is a pastor. Not only must he chart a course for his life, he must also lead his church in the direction it will go. A pastor needs guidance on a regular basis on where to go with his preaching. Every preacher knows there are often weeks when he does not have a clue in which direction to go in message preparation. The psalmist wrote, *"I will instruct thee and teach thee in the way which thou shalt go: I will guide thee with mine eye,"* (Psalm 32:8). Nevertheless, as a pastor approaches the throne of grace seeking leading on what he should preach, the Lord will invariably give direction.

Even more delicate is studying a passage of Scripture and honestly not understanding its intent. There at times is more than one way a passage can be understood. Again, the resource of guidance is the Lord through prayer. Jesus promised, *"Howbeit when he, the Spirit of truth, is come, he will guide you into all truth,"* (John 16:13). By knocking at the throne of grace concerning a given portion of Scripture, *"it shall be opened unto you."* That is not to preclude careful study, proper hermeneutics, and exegesis. However, in seeking His guidance for rightly dividing the Word of truth, He will guide with His eye.

Pastors often need guidance in program decisions or policy direction. More than one church has gotten into deep trouble because someone unwisely charged ahead with an overly ambitious building program. Sometimes it is a pastor who has grandiose visions of an impressive church plant. Sometimes, it is a gung-ho committee enthusiastically charging ahead with building plans. Such plans usually involve borrowing money, and that is where churches get in trouble. The pastor may not be the final word in such matters, but he does carry much influence. Anytime such matters as building, borrowing, or moving are at hand, a pastor needs profound guidance from on high. That comes only as he approaches the throne of grace seeking such. The psalmist wrote, *"Thou shalt guide me with thy counsel,"* (Psalm 73:24).

The great promise in Proverbs 3:5-6 certainly applies to pastoral prayer. There the Holy Spirit wrote, *"Trust in the LORD with all thine heart; and lean not unto thine own understanding. In all thy ways acknowledge him, and he shall direct thy paths."* The essence is, in all of our decisions seek His face. Then He will direct our paths. The Hebrew word translated "acknowledge" (yada) is the same word commonly rendered as "to know." In other words, in all our pathways - the forks in the road of life - know the Lord. That is, seek His guidance. It is then, and only then, *"he shall direct thy paths."* That, incidentally, is an act of faith which is part of living by faith.

My father had a basic axiom. Whenever there were serious decisions to be made, he would take the matter to the Lord in prayer. He continuously sought guidance from the Chief Shepherd. Such counsel is never wrong.

4. **Strength** - Do pastors ever get discouraged? Well, anyone who has ever held that sacred office knows the answer to that. It may be trouble in the church. A disloyal deacon or staff member may be subtly undercutting the pastor. It is discouraging. There come business meetings which are unsettling. It may be an open flare-up over the least predictable concern. It may be a pastor's intuition telling him though people didn't cause trouble in the meeting, they really weren't with him. His intuition may tell him a split is coming. It is disheartening. Though sometimes it is good for a church to eliminate problem people, it is always disheartening to a pastor. Over the years, we have had people leave the church for one reason or another. After the dust had settled and time had passed, it was evident the departure of some certainly was for the best. But I will

guarantee that it is disheartening for a pastor nevertheless, as it takes place.

It may be the attendance is down. That can take the wind out of any pastor's sails. It may be the offerings are not meeting the budget. That is demoralizing. I have known more than one pastor who has had his paycheck reduced or even eliminated because the church was undergoing a financial crisis. That is discouraging. I have known churches which either were on the brink of foreclosure or actually entered into receivership. That will take the starch out of a pastor. There are endless ways trouble, concerns, and anxieties may arise. A veteran pastor can intuitively sense when people are not with him. He can see it in their eyes. He can detect it in their demeanor. It is troubling. It is disheartening.

I once received an advertisement for a particular pastors' fellowship meeting. The essence was how I needed this meeting to be strengthened and encouraged in the ministry. Maybe that is what took place at that meeting. I don't know. I did not go. However, I would suggest a resource of strength and encouragement which is always available. One need not spend money to receive it. One need not wait until a special conference or meeting is held. One need not travel to find it. It is going to the Lord and finding strength and encouragement on one's knees. Isaiah the prophet wrote, "*But they that wait upon the LORD, shall renew their strength,*" (Isaiah 40:31). The strength to which Isaiah wrote in its most basic form is encouragement. God is able to strengthen us physically. But the help which only He can give comes as we wait upon Him. That in considerable measure comes as we spend time before the throne of grace. There is nothing more refreshing spiritually than a sweet hour of prayer. Over the years, this preacher has had his batteries recharged many times while spending time with the Strength of my life. Space does not allow us to track all that Scripture has to say about being strengthened. Yet briefly, it comes from the Author of strength. David wrote, "*The LORD is the strength of my life,*" (Psalm 27:1). Isaiah wrote, "*The LORD JEHOVAH is my strength,*" (Isaiah

12:2). Paul spoke of *"the God of all comfort"* in II Corinthians 1:3. The word translated "comfort" or "consolation" in II Corinthians 1 is "paraklaysis." In modern vernacular, it has the simple sense of encouragement. God is the God of all encouragement. Why seek strength and encouragement from secondary sources when the ultimate source is freely available?

As a pastor spends time alone with the Lord of Glory, some of that radiance will begin to lift his spirit. Though there are many problems and discouragements in the ministry, He gives strength as we seek it. David, the veteran warrior wrote, *"For thou hast girded me with strength unto the battle,"* (Psalm 18:39). Spend time alone with Him in prayer. Giving strength is one of His specialties. Moreover, His strength never fails. That strength is found as a pastor meets Him at the throne of grace.

5. Help - A closely related necessity in serving the King is finding help in time of need. One pastor has commented, there were times in his ministry he was so low, he had to reach up to touch bottom. Crises come in the ministry. Problems crop up which seem insurmountable. They may be of a financial nature. They may be personal in nature. They may seem impossible to overcome. As the little chorus says, however, "God specializes in things thought impossible." That help comes almost exclusively as we get alone in prayer before the throne of grace. As one famous preacher once said, "All our failures are prayer failures." James wrote, *"Ye have not because ye ask not,"* (James 4:3). I am aware of a church which literally ran out of money. The pastor and his assistant could no longer be paid. Yet, as they went to their knees and besought the Lord, a large check appeared in the offering one Sunday well into five digits. God helped them. But they first had to pray it down.

The Psalmist wrote, *"LORD, be thou my helper,"* Psalm 30:10. The Bible is full of stories where God intervened and miraculously helped His people as they besought Him in prayer. Recall the story of Peter in prison awaiting execution. The church literally prayed him out. Recall also the story of the Shunammite woman whose son had died. As Elijah prayed, God restored the boy to life. The same God is still on the throne. He still helps His people as they cry out to Him. The psalmist wrote, *"Ye that fear the LORD, trust in the LORD: he is their help and their shield,"* (Psalm 115:11).

I am mindful of a preacher who was told by his doctor he had six months to live. He was sick, and he knew it. Nevertheless, he sought help from God according to James 5:14-15. He asked that prayer according to James 5:14 be made over him on the platform of the church in a public service. That preacher is still going. God healed him years ago. God helped him as he sought help through prayer.

Legion are the stories of God helping His people as they besought Him in prayer. Pastors will come up against brick walls. There seems no way through the obstacle. There is no way around it, over it, or under it. But as help is sought from the throne of grace, God can and will solve the problem. One of the great privileges in serving the King is the unlimited help from Him available in time of need. It is only as far away as our prayer closet.

6. Intercession - The very nature of a pastoral ministry is such that a pastor is aware of the problems and needs of numerous people. It is incumbent upon a pastor to pray for them. Though in a somewhat different context, Samuel cried, *"God forbid that I should sin against the LORD in ceasing to pray for you,"* (I Samuel 12:23). Even as Samuel had been given spiritual oversight of Israel, pastors are given the spiritual oversight of churches today. One of the great quantities of prayer in a pastor's prayer life ought to be interceding for his people. I well recall finding my father praying over the membership list of the church on numerous occasions. He prayed for each person by name systematically.

Men in the church would come to him for prayer as they faced times of need in their lives. I recall one brother who came to pray with his pastor on a regular basis. His business was young and fragile. He had mortgaged his house against it. Everything he owned was tied up in that business. There were several times he came to Dad for prayer and said, "If the Lord doesn't do something by tomorrow, I will be out of business." They would kneel down together in Dad's study and pray for deliverance. The Lord always came through. For some years it was touch and go in that man's business. Times were hard, but God pulled him through. As the years have passed, God has blessed that man, and his business has flourished. He came to his pastor seeking fervent prayer on his behalf, and God honored such faith.

There are endless needs people have of which a pastor can and ought to intercede in prayer. There are loved ones connected with the church who are not saved. Wives have unsaved husbands. In some cases, the reverse is the case. They need prayer. A perceptive pastor will be aware of people who are back slidden. He ought to pray for them. There are young Christians in the church. They need prayer. The youth of the church are at constant risk from attack of the devil. They need prayer. There are often people of the church who are seriously ill, even to the point of death. There are men in the church who are unemployed and facing hard times. There are wayward young people of good parents. There are young men in the church who have sensed God's call to the ministry. Missionaries need prayer. There is no end to the list of people who have needs for which a pastor can pray.

The Chief Shepherd has set an example for us. He *"even is at the right hand of God, who maketh intercession for us,"* (Romans 8:34). If our Savior is interceding on our behalf, it follows His under-shepherds ought do the same. The ministry of Paul was replete with intercessory prayer as noted earlier. We also ought to do the same.

7. **Provision** - James wrote, *"Ye have not because ye ask not,"* (James 4:3). There are always financial or material needs in God's work. Early in my ministry, I assumed a pastorate which was in a financial crisis. The leadership of the church did not inform their newly called pastor of the total crisis until after he had accepted the call and had arrived. The only real solution was to pray for God's provision. The entire church was admonished to pray. Within three months, the immediate crisis had passed, and within a year it largely

had been alleviated. More than anything else, it was prayer which resolved the crisis.

In starting a church, we saw God virtually give the church seven acres of land. But it had been brought before Him in prayer. In seeking permits to build upon that land, we discovered our plans were not in compliance with zoning and environmental regulations. Prayer caused the city to issue special-use permits and waive other restrictions. Prayer caused God to put it in the heart of the U.S. Army to level the land free of charge as a training exercise, saving the young church thousands of dollars. As we prayed, God took our five loaves and two fishes' worth of resources and stretched it into a handsome new church building. To this day, people comment upon the beauty of it. Others stop and ask if they can take pictures of it. But God provided as His people prayed.

I am convinced there are no obstacles which cannot be removed, or lack which cannot be met if a pastor and his people will pray. Paul wrote to the Philippian church assuring them, *"But my God shall supply your need according to his riches in glory by Christ Jesus,"* (Philippians 4:19). The linkage for the fulfillment of that promise is prayer. The pastor ought to be out in front leading the church in this regard.

8. Wisdom - If there is anything a pastor needs, it is wisdom. Solomon wrote an entire book stressing the importance of wisdom. In Proverbs 4:5 he wrote, *"Get wisdom, get understanding: forget it not; neither decline from the words of my mouth."* Then in verse 7, he wrote, *"Wisdom is the principal thing; therefore get wisdom: and with all thy getting get understanding."* Job wrote earlier, *"But where shall wisdom be found? And where is the place of understanding?"* (Job 28:12). An entire book could be written in response to that question. However, James gave a simple answer: *"If any of you lack wisdom, let him ask of God, that giveth to all men liberally, and upbraideth not; and it shall be given him,"* (James 1:5). God gives wisdom as we pray and seek it.

Pray without Ceasing!

Pastors are confronted continuously with matters requiring wisdom for proper resolution. There are policy decisions which must be made. Not only is the essence of a policy crucial, but often the timing of it. Wisdom is needed. Every church has problem people. It takes wisdom in knowing how to handle them. Problems crop up, often unexpectedly, requiring immediate attention. A pastor needs wisdom in dealing with them. People call or approach a pastor with questions he may not be prepared to answer on the spot. He needs wisdom not only in answering the question itself but also in *how* to defer the matter if needed. People are sensitive. A word out of place or the tone in which it is said can offend those who are prone thereto. A pastor needs wisdom in deporting himself. It is one thing for a pastor to carefully prepare a message to be delivered. It is another thing to have someone drop a loaded question on him as he walks down the hall before or after a service. Part of the daily prayer regimen of a pastor ought to be seeking wisdom. It is crucial.

Henry Sorenson was a man of prayer. He knew how to pray. He was a regular and frequent supplicant at the throne of grace. From his time in prayer came fellowship with the Savior. It was the source of his power in preaching. He found guidance, strength, and help therefrom. He endlessly interceded for others and their needs. And as he spent time with the Giver of Wisdom, he found wisdom for the problems in the ministry. Paul wrote Pastor Timothy, "*I will therefore that men pray everywhere, lifting up holy hands, without wrath and doubting,*" (I Timothy 2:8). Of all people, that admonition starts with pastors.

Chapter 10 - A Servant's Heart

"Not to be ministered unto, but to minister"

A minister is a servant. A common concept in the Bible is that of servants. It is not particularly common in our Western, democratic culture. Nevertheless, the matter of servants or of serving (sometimes called ministering) appears over one thousand times in the Bible. Needless to say, it is endemic to the biblical context and culture and not to ours. In the Scripture, there were a number of degrees of servitude, but all implied a greater or lesser degree of inferiority and a lack of liberty. One of the most common usages of the idea in the Bible is that of a slave. That is the essence of the Greek word "doulos" which is used approximately 120 times in the New Testament. (It also at times carried the idea of a hired workman.) Other ideas are of being a subordinate to or serving another. In all cases, the greater idea is of submission and service for others.

A colloquial synonym for a pastor is a "minister." People, particularly of an older generation, often refer to a pastor as their minister. And, the overall work of a pastor is referred to as "the

The Art of Pastoring

ministry." The English word "minister" is a synonym for a servant. In the New Testament, the two terms are used virtually interchangeably. To serve is to minister and vice versa. As I visit in the homes of particularly older people, they often will refer to me as either "their" minister or "the" minister. Such usage is slowly fading as that generation fades. Nevertheless, it reflects a biblical principle. A pastor is a minister. He ought to be a servant and have the heart of a servant.

In the Greek New Testament, the various scriptural penmen used seven different words which all are translated as "servant" or in some cases, "minister." Three of these are miscellaneous words with minimal usage. However, four words are used significantly, referring to service or ministering. The most frequently used word for servant is "doulos." Its sense ranges from a hired employee to a bond slave. The latter is its most basic sense. Another word frequently translated as "servant" or "minister" is "diakonos." It also is translated as "deacon." Its basic sense is that of a servant. However, if there is a nuance of distinction, it referred more narrowly to those involved with serving food. A third relatively common word is "huperetes." It literally means an "under-rower" as on a galley ship. However, it had the common usage of an officer such as a mid-rank officer on a ship and is translated as "officer" a number of times. It also is translated as "minister." To a lesser degree, the word "leitourgos" is translated as "minister." It had the sense of a public servant such as a governmental "minister." It also was used in regard to the service of the temple. However, in every case, each of these words has the sense of serving or doing the will of another.

Not to be ministered unto but to minister. For years, my father had printed on his calling cards that which Jesus said, *"Not to be ministered unto, but to minister,"* (Matthew 20:28, also Mark 10:45). That simple quote accurately described his ministry. As far as Dad was concerned, God had called him to serve the people he pastored and then some. He subordinated his life and career to serving others. His first ministry was to the One who had saved him

A Servant's Heart

and placed him in His service. Then, his ministry diffused outward to serve those who called him "pastor." Finally, he was a servant to anyone else who came seeking help from a "minister" of Jesus Christ.

In the culture in which we live, servitude is viewed as lowly rank. Moreover, in terms of human rights or civil rights, to be a servant or slave is abhorrent to the politically-correct mind. Yet, God views such service highly. Being a servant of God is a high estate indeed. It has esteemed company. Most of the apostles referred to themselves as servants. For example, Peter began his second epistle by referring to himself as "*Simon Peter, a servant and an apostle of Jesus Christ,*" (II Peter 1:1). James called himself "*a servant of God and of the Lord Jesus Christ,*" (James 1:1). Jude noted how he was "*the servant of Jesus Christ,*" (Jude 1). John, in his characteristic modesty, refers to himself in relation to Jesus Christ as "*his servant John,*" (Revelation 1:1). Paul similarly so referred to himself in Romans 1:1 ("*Paul, a servant of Jesus Christ*") and Titus 1:1 ("*Paul a servant of God and an apostle of Jesus Christ*").

To minister involves serving people. It is relatively easy to think of oneself as a servant of God or of Christ. There the distinction of the Superior One versus the inferior is self-evident. In many ways, it is a title of privilege to be called a servant of God. However, the area where some become reluctant to think of themselves as servants is in relation to other people. It has been my experience, some in the ministry have a practical problem with such a concept. After all, *the* pastor holds an important position. He is *the* head of the only body Jesus Christ established on this earth, the local church. The mission of the church is the most important mission in the world. He may have a number of paid assistants and subordinates who report to him. He likes being called "Pastor," "the Pastor," or "Reverend." He is part of that elite fraternity called "the clergy." He gets special parking rights at the hospital and has a special cloakroom there. The directors of the local funeral homes treat him like a king. Hundreds of people come to hear him speak each week. He even has a special parking spot near the door of the church. He chairs important committee meetings. Few people dare to cross him. He is *the* pastor.

It is a "given," he is a servant of God. However, it is easy for him to ignore the idea of being a servant to other people. He would rather view himself as the chief executive officer of the church. He has instructed his secretary to intercept anyone trying to see him without an appointment. He has become a little aloof, and, correspondingly, his hat size has inflated some. Yet the Bible clearly teaches, those in the ministry are to be servants of *men*.

The Example of Paul

Your servant for Jesus' sake. The Apostle Paul wrote how *"though I be free from all men, yet have I made myself servant unto all,"* (II Corinthians 9:19). Though Paul had free status under Roman law and hence was not legally a slave, nevertheless, he had humbled himself to be a servant to all men. There is an inherent humility in voluntary servitude. When Paul wrote to the church at Corinth the second time, he made the comment how he and Timothy were *their* servants for Jesus' sake (II Corinthians 4:5). Paul viewed himself as a servant of the church. When he wrote the church at Rome, he made mention how he planned to *"go unto Jerusalem to minister unto the saints,"* (Romans 15:25). The word translated "minister" here is "diakoneo" which literally means to serve or to be a servant. Again, the great apostle viewed himself as a servant. His framework of life was to serve others.

Indeed, when Jesus Christ appeared to him on the road to Damascus provoking his conversion, He made an interesting comment to Paul. As Paul lay prostrate on the road already blinded by the glory of the resurrected Christ, Jesus said to him, *"But rise, and stand upon thy feet: for I have appeared unto thee for this purpose, to make thee a **minister** and a witness,"* (Acts 26:16). As noted earlier, the word translated "minister" here is "hyperertes." Its literal sense was "an under-rower" as on a galley ship. However, it had come to have the general idea of being a servant or subordinate officer. In so many words, Jesus said to Paul, "I have appeared unto thee to make thee a servant." Paul already was a rising star in the Pharisee party of Judaism. Though relatively young, he very possibly may already have been a member of the Jewish Sanhedrin, the highest office in Roman-occupied Israel. He was highly educated. He came from a prominent Jewish family from the Hellenist city of Tarsus. He was a free-born, Roman citizen, no small rank in first-century, Roman culture.

Now the One whom he had hated and persecuted had confronted him in such power and glory, he could only submit to Him, trusting Him as his Lord and Savior. And now the Resurrected One informed him how He had appeared unto him to make him a *servant*! It must have been a day which shocked Paul to the center of his being. Yet, from that day onward, he never wavered. He willingly became not only a servant of Jesus Christ his Savior, he also humbled himself to become a servant unto all who named the name of Christ. The simple truth is, Paul had a great example.

The Example of Jesus

God's servant. Jesus Christ is referred to in several places as a servant. As the Holy Spirit moved the prophet Zechariah, he wrote, "*Behold, I will bring forth my servant the BRANCH,*" (Zechariah 3:8). The context is clearly of the coming Messiah. Even before that, God through the prophet Isaiah had written concerning the coming Anointed One, "*Behold my servant, in whom I uphold; mine elect, in whom my soul delighteth; I have put my spirit upon him: he shall bring forth judgment to the Gentiles,*" (Isaiah 42:1). The context unquestionably is that of Christ. But Jehovah God called him "my Servant." Again in Isaiah 52:13, the coming Messiah is noted. There, the prophet wrote, "*Behold, my servant shall deal prudently, he shall be exalted and extolled, and be very high.*" It seems paradoxical. He who is King of Kings is called a servant.

Nevertheless, in His earthly ministry, He taught His disciples, *"And whosoever will be chief among you, let him be your **servant**: even as the Son of man came not to be ministered unto, but to minister, and to give his life a ransom for many,"* (Matthew 20:27-28). For indeed, He *"made himself of no reputation, and took upon him the form of a servant, and was made in the likeness of men . . . wherefore God also hath highly exalted him, and given him a name which is above every name,"* (Philippians 2:7,9). Jesus humbled himself and became a servant - first to His heavenly Father, and then for us. Without question, there is no higher company than that of our Lord. Yet, He became a servant;. He had a servant's heart. To follow in His footsteps and be a servant as well is of high degree.

A leader must be a servant. In the days just prior to Jesus' crucifixion, the mother of two of His disciples (the sons of Zebedee - James and John) came to Him and asked her sons be granted positions of rank in Christ's coming kingdom. When the other ten heard about that, it stirred indignation. In that context, Jesus commented, *"Ye know that the princes of the Gentiles exercise dominion over them, and they that are great exercise authority upon them. But it shall not be so among you:* ***but whosoever will be great among you, let him be your minister; and whosoever will be chief among you, let him be your servant****,"* (Matthew 20:25-27). The word translated "minister" is "diakonos" and means a waiter or servant. When Jesus spoke of one being "chief," the word used is "protos" and means "first." The final word "servant" is translated from "doulos," the Greek term for the lowest level of servant, i.e., a slave. In other words, what Jesus taught His disciples is this: if one wishes to be the leader, then let him be a servant. Or, if one desires to be the number one man, let him humble himself and become a lowly servant. Moreover, Jesus was not advancing the idea how starting as a servant was the recommended route for promotion. Rather, He taught, that a leader must *be* a servant. That is the antithesis of how the world goes about doing things (i.e., *"they that are great exercise authority over them"*).

A Servant's Heart

The pastor is the leader of the church. He is the number one man, as it were. He is the one who occupies the "big" chair on the church platform. Jesus taught that the leader therefore must become a servant to those he leads. It is part of the job description of being a spiritual leader. He taught a similar truth in Matthew 23:10-11, *"Neither be ye called masters: for one is your Master, even Christ. But he that is greatest among you shall be your servant."* Jesus demonstrated His own servant's heart later that week when He washed His disciples' feet, wiping them with a towel at the last supper. That was a job typically reserved for a servant. The whole business of foot washing was Jesus' exhibiting a servant's heart. He was not establishing another ordinance for the coming church. Rather, he was presenting an example how His disciples ought to have a servant's heart in their coming ministries.

Down through the years, my father on occasion served as church janitor. At times, it was to supplement his salary. At other times, there was no one else willing to do it. But if there was a task which needed to be done, he was willing to do it. After he retired, he joined with me in helping get a new church established. After the young church had built its first building, Dad volunteered to become the janitor of the new building. There was no fanfare made about it. He just quietly took care of the building. The people of the church knew something about Dad. They knew he had a Doctor of Divinity degree. They knew he had pastored a church which at one time had approximately one thousand people. They knew he had had a fruitful ministry. One day, a man of the church was driving by the church building and saw Dad's car parked there alone. So the fellow turned into the parking lot and went in to talk to him. The building was quiet, and no one seemed to be inside, so the man called out for Dr. Sorenson. As he walked down a corridor, he heard him reply, "I'm in here." The man entered into the men's room, and there to his amazement was Dr. Henry Sorenson on his knees cleaning the toilets. It astounded him. But it should not have. The Bible teaches how a pastor ought to be a servant. Dad was not too important to clean toilets, or do such menial work as being a janitor. He had a servant's heart.

In the same context of the last supper and the washing of His disciples' feet, Jesus said, *"Verily, verily, I say unto you, The servant is not greater than his lord; neither is he that is sent greater than he that sent him. If ye know these things, happy are ye if ye do them,"* (John 13:16-17). An insight into happiness is found. As we humble ourselves and become servants, we will find our ministry to be far happier than if we don't.

Someday when we stand before our Lord as His undershepherds, what an honor it will be to hear him say, *"Well done, thou good and faithful servant: thou hast been faithful over a few things, I will make thee ruler over many things,"* (Matthew 25:21). The use of the term "servant" is not accidental. We have been called to be servants both to God and of them we lead.

Timothy, as a pastor, was called to be a servant. Paul wrote Timothy warning him of the coming apostasy. He urged him to *"put the brethren in remembrance of these things,"* (I Timothy 4:6). But then he wrote, how in so doing, Timothy would therefore *"be a good minister of Jesus Christ."* The word translated "minister" once again is "diakonos." It conveys the idea of being a waiter or servant. The point simply is how Timothy, as pastor, was called to be a servant. In a similar vein, Paul wrote Pastor Timothy in his second epistle and instructed him how *"the servant of the Lord must not strive; but be gentle unto all men, apt to teach patient,"* (II Timothy 2:24). That includes being gentle (good natured), apt to teach (willing and ready to teach others), and patient (with those who may be otherwise aggravating). Not only is a pastor a servant of God and of the church he serves, his very attitude must be one which is cooperative, patient with people, and willing to help them.

In looking back over my father's ministry, he was always willing and ready to help people. As noted earlier, his planned day-off was never used to side-step someone who came seeking his assistance. He cut vacations short to minister to his people. He was at their bedside

A Servant's Heart

at all hours of the day or night, if needed. Growing up in his parsonage, I know he took phone calls all hours of the night and often arose to go and help someone in need. Henry Sorenson had a servant's heart. He served his Savior. He served the church he pastored. He served the people of the church in whatever their need. That service was not just spiritual in nature. There were many menial, physical tasks he just quietly did. He took care of the church plant. He oversaw its property. He helped people financially on numerous occasions. I know for a fact, he loaned considerable sums of money to people in the church in their time of need. Unfortunately, more than one of those loans became a gift because the party never repaid it. But Dad's spirit was to serve them in any way he could. He truly came not to be ministered unto, but to minister.

Chapter 11 - Flies in the Ointment

"Dead flies cause the ointment of the apothecary to send for a stinking savour."

A little foolishness can ruin a pastor's ministry. In Ecclesiastes 10:1, there is a remarkable principle. Someone in leadership can ruin his ministry by a little foolishness. Solomon wrote, *"Dead flies cause the ointment of the apothecary to send forth a stinking savour: so doth a little folly him that is in reputation for wisdom and honour."* Many a man has either washed out of the ministry or had his ministry damaged by folly. The scriptural writer used a simple illustration of life to form a simple proverb.

Ancient apothecaries prepared expensive, anointing oils and ointments made from olive oil and oriental spices. However, when flies got stuck and died, the costly preparation would putrefy and begin to stink. Such a small corruption as dead flies could ruin an otherwise valuable preparation. And so it is in the ministry. A little imprudence can do grave damage to one's ministry. A pastor certainly is one in reputation for wisdom and honor.

The Art of Pastoring

Having been in the ministry for almost thirty years, I have witnessed men who were good pastors, good preachers, good soul winners, and good administrators have their ministry damaged by some seemingly minor problem. In many cases, such folly has forced pastors to seek another place of service. In some cases, it has knocked them out the ministry altogether.

Unfortunately, it does not take a great deal of folly to damage one's reputation. Indeed, a good name is better than precious ointment. It is rather to be chosen than great riches. A little carelessness, a little indiscretion, little habits, or little character defects will sooner or later catch up with a man and mar his reputation. A man may have been to the best of colleges or seminaries. He may be completely orthodox doctrinally. He may have a right philosophy of the ministry and be in the best of fellowships. But foolishness can hurt his ministry for a long time thereafter. An improper ranking of priorities can suddenly catch up. Long standing character flaws which have been glossed over and long swept under the rug can suddenly become a source of great chagrin. Shortcuts in Christian living sooner or later catch up. Compromises of separation or integrity sooner or later surface. Moral failure will inevitably come to the light of day. Therefore, it is incumbent upon any man either in a pastoral ministry or aspiring thereof to strive endlessly for integrity, maturity, and righteous character. To tolerate anything less will eventually unravel one's own ministry.

Let us consider ten types of "flies" which can foul the reputation of a pastor's ministry. Though some of these certainly are more serious than others, even the seemingly inconsequential flaws can have serious repercussions.

1. Loss of Temper - A New Testament word often translated as "wrath" is "thumos" and has the idea of a boiled-over temper. For example, the apostle wrote, *"But now ye also put off all these . . . anger,"* (Colossians 3:8). I have known pastors down through the years who at times did not discipline their emotions. One preacher was an avid softball and baseball player. I will call him Pastor Boyle. He always was on the church team. However, he became renowned for his loss of temper in church-league games. If the umpire made a call he thought was wrong, he quickly would "go ballistic." Just like unregenerate ball players in the world, Pastor Boyle could fly into a rage challenging the official. He would throw his hat on the ground, stomp around, and argue nose to nose with the umpire. He became oblivious to how everyone else at the game viewed him. He was mad. He was steamed. And, he did not care who knew it.

Players from other churches were embarrassed. The umpires knew he was the pastor of the church. His own team was embarrassed. People from his own church came away with eroded respect for their pastor. He would later apologize, but the damage had been done. It was like trying to unring a bell. The umpire and other players could accept his apology and forgive him on their part. Even a public apology to the church could smooth things over only temporarily. The people had learned their pastor would not control his temper.

That same character defect later showed up in other settings. One day, a Sunday School teacher in the church crossed the pastor on a matter of policy. Technically, he was right, and she was wrong. But in the ensuing confrontation, he lost his temper. He later apologized. However, the damage was done. Not only did that particular family soon leave the church, the incident became known in the congregation. The confidence of the people was further eroded in their pastor. In one particular deacons' meeting, several men took a position which was in opposition to that of the pastor. In the subsequent discussion, the pastor again did not control his temper. Statements were made. Things were said, and further damage was done to the respect people had for their pastor. Someone once said, "He who makes an enemy out of an adversary is a fool." This pastor was perilously close to that position.

Things quickly went from bad to worse. A faction within the church took the position either the pastor ought to leave or they would, splitting the church. The pastor wrestled with the matter and before long resigned. He was sound in doctrine. He had a proper philosophy of the ministry. He was a good preacher and a good soul winner. He had helped the church go forward in attendance and growth. However, the dead fly of not controlling his temper began to cause his ministry to have an unseemly odor. It undercut the confidence and respect his congregation had for him. He tried to defend himself by saying it was just his emotional temperament. That may have been true, but it did not alter the fact such behavior had damaged his ministry. Though his temperament might have been inclined to such outbursts, that did not preclude him from changing habits and inclinations. It was the fly in the ointment of his ministry.

2. **Being undisciplined** - Paul wrote how *"every man that striveth for the mastery is temperate in all things,"* (I Corinthians 9:25). The essence of Christian character is the self-discipline to do what is right. I have known numbers of men in the ministry who failed largely because they were undisciplined. I think of a pastor I will call "Pastor Bob." He was a genuinely godly man. He loved the Lord. In his convictions, he held the highest of standards, at least as far as outward appearance was concerned. He had a burning desire to serve the Lord. He truly had sacrificed to be in the ministry. He was sound in doctrine. He had a burden for the lost. He had a good education from good schools. He was talented. And, he was a nice guy.

However, Pastor Bob had a glaring weakness. It was not obvious in first meeting him. In fact, it did not surface until people had worked with him for a while. He was undisciplined. Hudson Taylor once said, "An undisciplined man will never amount to anything in God's work." Sadly, that axiom was true for Pastor Bob. He would wait until the last moment to plan details. He often was tardy. Sometimes, he forgot important matters. Therefore, his execution and administration of church affairs were often ragged. He would wait until the eleventh hour in preparing messages. At times, because other things had gone wrong from lack of foresight and preparation, he was so tied up in knots trying to catch up on other pressing matters that even at the eleventh hour there was not time to get a message ready. A pastor can fake it a little while, but soon his people began to pick up on his being unprepared in the pulpit. It was easy to schedule Christian films in lieu of preaching. It was easier to have a missionary in the pulpit than for him to preach.

Details such as special speakers showing up whom he had forgotten were coming began to erode the confidence of his people. Because he failed to think ahead, things were often planned at the last minute. His people became weary of having a fellowship this Saturday announced for the first time at the mid-week service. They noticed how details in the church bulletin were often inaccurate. Pastor Bob did not have his act together because he was personally undisciplined. As people had the opportunity to view his car in the church parking lot, they noticed it always looked like the inside of a garbage dumpster. It always was visibly a mess. They noticed how Pastor Bob was perennially in financial distress. He confided to one of his deacons how he never had time to balance or reconcile his checkbook. His deacons noticed how he seemed to have the same attitude toward church finances. If there was money in the church treasury, he wanted to spend it.

Pastor Bob's people little by little lost confidence in his leadership. They liked him as a person. They respected his stand on matters of principle and conviction. However, they saw much inconsistency in day-to-day matters of character such as being on time, being organized, being on top of details, and doing things properly. Pastor Bob tried to pass it off, claiming he was a "people person." His "gift" was in dealing with people. Somebody else could sweat the details. Well, being a "people-person" can be a benefit, but it is no excuse for being undisciplined, unorganized, and undependable.

Pastor Bob's root problem lay in that he was mentally lazy. It was easy to pursue things he wanted to pursue. It was mental work to sit down, think ahead, foresee the problems and needs coming, plan for those needs, and then organize what needed to be done. Therefore, he waited until the last minute. Accordingly, his planning, organization, and programs were usually half-baked and half-cocked. His people noticed that and lost confidence in his leadership. It was easier to shoot the breeze on the telephone than sit down and prepare a message. Therefore, he procrastinated. It was easier to go to a pastors' fellowship than sit down and plan events for the church. It was easier to "fellowship" with others over coffee than tend to organizational details of church administration.

Pastor Bob's lack of discipline began to erode his ministry. People in the church became disenchanted with the frequent bungles of organization. They became frustrated by his lack of preparation. Some began to leave the church and go elsewhere. Others became distant, no longer supporting their pastor. Church finances became tight. There came months when there was not enough funds to pay Pastor Bob a full paycheck. Finally, several deacons met with him and suggested he begin to look elsewhere. His mental laziness which underlaid his lack of discipline and manifested itself in endless gaffs, bungles, and oversights had completely unraveled the confidence of the church in his ministry. Pastor Bob was frustrated, discouraged, and ready to quit the ministry. He would not acknowledge how his life-long pattern of following the path of least resistance had virtually ruined his ministry. It was a dead fly in the ointment of his ministry.

3. **Pride and Stubbornness** - Solomon wrote, *"Pride goeth before destruction, and an haughty spirit before a fall,"* (Proverbs 16:18). Pride in the ministry is like cancer. It often goes unnoticed until there suddenly is a major problem. However, like cancer, pride will eat away at the spiritual vitality of a pastor's ministry. It will erode the confidence of his people. Without a question, God is unimpressed with pride on our part.

I will call him Pastor Ron. He had graduated from a well-thought-of Christian college. He had received a graduate degree from a good post-theological graduate program. He held a good doctrinal position. He took a good stand on vital issues of the day. He certainly held good fundamental credentials. Moreover, Pastor Ron was talented in a number of areas, and he knew it. He had good ideas and sought to implement them. However, when a godly deacon made a suggestion concerning a change in a particular program, Pastor Ron ignored it. Time passed, and another loyal deacon suggested a similar adjustment in the program of the church. Pastor Ron just brushed off the idea. Both of these good, godly deacons were put off by how the pastor essentially ignored their suggestions. On another occasion, a woman in a position of leadership in the church stopped the pastor in the hall and asked if she could ask a question. The pastor said, "Sure." The pastor could sense the woman did not totally agree with his position. Therefore, he let it be known he had not only a bachelor's degree in Bible, but also a master's degree. The woman felt she had been put down by her pastor. Little by little, people began to compare notes on how the pastor would not take advice or listen to even constructive criticism.

Though Pastor Ron was a good man, he also was headstrong. His pride and stubbornness were eating away at the good will and confidence his people placed in him. Unfortunately, it began to unravel his position of leadership. He did not even realize it. However, things unfortunately came to a head one night in a tense deacons' meeting. All of the pent-up frustration and offense erupted in a most unpleasant meeting. The pastor came away stunned. He had no idea people harbored such negative feelings. He was discouraged. His first temptation was to blame those who delivered the bad news. They must be disloyal. They must be undermining him. Fortunately for Pastor Ron, he slowly realized he had provoked most of the trouble himself. It was a hard pill to swallow. Moreover, it took time - a long time - for the people to forget. But he painfully worked at doing better.

The Art of Pastoring

4. Laziness - Proverbs 20:4 says, "*The sluggard will not plow by reason of the cold.*" The Hebrew word translated "sluggard" essentially means "lazy." In all candor, this author can think of few terms more insulting than to be called lazy. It is an appalling way to talk about someone else. Yet, it is a problem in the ministry. Evangelists travel across the country and observe many churches and pastors. One day while talking with an evangelist friend, the comment was made how three things can destroy a man in the ministry: money, morals, and malice. The evangelist went on to say, "I can add a fourth: laziness." Most have heard the old joke about several little boys talking. One said, "My dad is a fireman." The next said, "My dad is a policeman." Then they turned to the other little boy and asked, "What does your dad do?" He replied, "He doesn't do anything. He's a preacher." All too often people in the world have the idea a pastor speaks on Sunday and then has the rest of the time off. Anyone who has been around a Bible-believing church will know the opposite is more the truth. Many pastors will put in sixty to eighty hours a week. Yet, there are those who do goof off.

Pastor Wellstone "religiously" took each Monday as his day off. On a regular week day, he often didn't drift into the office until 10 a.m. or later. He often took long lunches. He was always game for golf. He could usually think of excuses for not putting more time in pastoral visitation. He always jumped at the opportunity to go to pastors' fellowships or retreats. He made a point to go to camp with his young people for several weeks each summer, though he had no real duties there. And by all means, he could not miss the annual week-long meetings of the association. Moreover, he always took his vacations to the max. He had his secretary take care of much of the administrative details of the church because he was so "busy."

His people noticed how their pastor was often not available when they would call. They noticed his car at the mall or restaurant parking lots at all waking hours. But he was a good guy and got along well with everyone. However, his church never saw any growth. Few people got saved through its ministry. Moreover, Pastor

Flies in the Ointment

Wellstone was not renowned for the depth of his sermons or lessons. The church seemed stagnant. To Pastor Wellstone, his position was basically a job. He preached weekly, married and buried as the need arose, and made visits at the hospital as needed. The rest of the time, he found other things to occupy his interests. Nobody was particularly upset with him. However, his penchant for laziness was a dead fly in the ointment which produced mediocrity not only of his personal ministry but also of his church. They together more or less faded into ecclesiastical oblivion.

5. Distractions - The very nature of the pastorate is such a pastor is for the most part his own boss. There are limitations upon that to be sure. However, a pastor can usually set his own schedule and priorities. Unfortunately, some pastors get side-tracked into secondary interests which distract them from their primary calling. Let us look at three somewhat typical distractions which have become dead flies in the ointment of some men and their ministries.

Business sidelines. Pastor Daschle liked to tinker with old cars. He found by buying certain types of older vehicles and restoring them in his spare time, he could sell them for a handsome profit. It was a fun diversion from the pressures of the ministry, and he supplemented his income in so doing. Moreover, he rationalized how Paul had made tents on the side to support himself in the ministry. He considered his car restoration operation to be a little tent-making sideline. As time passed, he found his hobby becoming a business. The profits were excellent. He had an eye for picking the right vehicle to restore and make an excellent return. He became knowledgeable of this market and who would buy and sell such cars. So far so good.

However, as Pastor Daschle became more and more involved in his sideline, he was distracted from his primary calling, the ministry. His attention to church duties became perfunctory and his ministry slowly withered. He was counseled by men in the church to back off. Yet, he kept at it. He had become accustomed to the extra income. Little by little, his church waned. Five years later, he was out

The Art of Pastoring

of the ministry. The dead fly of distraction had fouled the ointment of his ministry.

Sports. Pastor Roemer loved sports. He had played varsity basketball throughout his high school and college years. As a youth pastor he had played church league basketball and joined any other league he could find. He was good. As he later became a senior pastor, he continued to get his exercise from basketball. He was an avid fan not only of basketball, but most other major sports. He was a walking sports encyclopedia. Because of his sports interest, he went down to a local radio station and met with the station manager. He offered the following deal. If the station would put a program from his church on free, in return, he would produce a sports-talk show for them. They agreed. It went over pretty good. He knew his sports stuff, and the church got a free weekly broadcast. Everybody was happy.

However, Pastor Roemer's love of sports was such he spent more and more time with them. He often was not around when people in the church needed him. He rarely visited in the homes of his people. He had become so busy, he was not available to pastor them. The people in the church little by little became put off by his sports mania. It came up in deacons' meetings. He apologized and agreed to be more circumspect. Yet, the draw was always there. Little by little, a chasm opened between Pastor Roemer and his people. Though he was the preacher, he really wasn't their pastor. He saw the handwriting on the wall and sought another church. The dead fly of a distraction was such that his ministry was seriously damaged.

Politics. Pastor Bowman was concerned about the political direction of the country. Therefore, he began to become involved in conservative, Republican party politics. He attended grass roots meetings and was elected to the county Republican convention. Because of his involvement on the county level, he was elected to the state convention. Since he was an experienced public speaker, he was influential there. Local, conservative leaders foresaw an opportunity to make inroads in the coming election. A long-term, liberal incumbent was stepping down from the city council. Therefore, they approached Pastor Bowman about being the conservative candidate for the seat. It was a small city, and they assured him he would still have time to be the pastor of his church. Therefore, Pastor Bowman declared himself to be a family-values candidate for the city council.

The election campaign was furious. He had not expected the vitriolic character denigration he faced from local, liberal, political-action groups. But he figured the publicity, though at times quite negative, was good, bringing attention to him and his church. He won the election and was seated on the council. He was a voice of conservative and biblical philosophy, though the liberal faction was pretty well able to thwart him politically. He found himself spending long hours dealing with policy matters. There were constant hours on the phone from backers and detractors in controversies. Though he had not wished to have his ministry diminished, that is exactly what happened. When he could have been out visiting people in the evening, there were never-ending council and committee meetings.

The long and short of it was, Pastor Bowman had become a figure-head pastor. Much of his time and interest had been diverted to the contentious politics of trying to reform his community. One evening, several deacons visited him and suggested he either resign from his political aspirations or resign the church. It was terribly embarrassing. He had bit off more than he could chew. He immediately resigned from neither. However, in the course of events, he eventually dropped out of the ministry altogether. He had lost the good will of the congregation where he was. The dead fly of distraction had caused the ointment of his ministry to stink.

6. One's wife- Solomon also wrote, *"He that findeth a wife findeth a good thing, and obtaineth favour of the LORD,"* (Proverbs 18:22). When this author was a seminary student years ago, a famous preacher came to speak in chapel and teach several classes. In one of the question-and-answer periods, someone asked what was the most important thing in a man's ministry. Without hesitation, the famous preacher shot back, "Your wife." He went on to counsel how for those men not yet married, the most important decision we would make would be that of a wife. After almost thirty years in the ministry, I must wholeheartedly agree. There is no question in my mind, whatever success I have had in the ministry has in considerable measure been augmented by my dear wife.

However, it has been my sad knowledge to know a number of pastors whose ministry was diminished or damaged because of their wives. For those reading this book still in college or seminary, believe this author. The most important choice a pastor will ever make for the ministry is the woman chosen to be his mate. It is sad when a pastor's wife unravels her husband's ministry, but it assuredly happens.

Some pastors' wives unfortunately gossip. Some have sharp tongues to other women in the church. Some are a poor testimony in their personal deportment or dress. Some nag and give their husbands grief for their long hours in the ministry. I think of a situation which unfortunately is all too typical.

Pastor Kohl's wife was very happy to be a pastor's wife. She liked the special attention and position it gave her in the church. She liked to be thought of as the first-lady of the church. She viewed herself as her husband's unofficial, yet nevertheless influential assistant. She assumed charge of the various departments in the church which were more oriented toward the women. She took charge of the music, the nursery, the social committee, and above all else, the flowers and decorations of the church. The women of the church came to realize, woe be to any women who crossed Mrs. Kohl. *Anything* which was done in those areas had to meet her approval. It didn't matter that other women in the church had taken care of those things over the years; she insisted on asserting her influence.

There came squabbles between her and ladies of the church. Her husband was fairly well-liked by the church in general, so it did not seem to affect his ministry too much. However, as Mrs. Kohl insisted upon her way, women of the church began to be put off. They came home unhappy campers, and that began to affect their husbands. Several men in the church went to Pastor Kohl and tried to discreetly talk to him about his wife. He immediately stuck up for her. The men left disheartened by the results of their meeting. Even worse, after that meeting, the wives of those men were noticeably snubbed by Mrs. Kohl. It only made matters worse.

One by one, the women of the church became unhappy. Several of them told their husbands they either wanted to look for another church or not go at all. Even some of the solid, stable deacons were shaken as their wives became frustrated. The upshot of it was, numbers of families did leave the church, even some of the pillars of the church. Moreover, the loss of those people put a noticeable dent in church finances. The dead fly of an unwise pastor's wife became a serious detraction to her husband's ministry.

7. **A CEO mentality** - Pastor McGovern was an outgoing personality. Much of the strength of his ministry lay in his gift of gab. He was a silver-tongued speaker not only in the pulpit but in personal conversation. He had had the opportunity to become the pastor of a large church. He was a gifted administrator and ran a tight ship. Yet for all his talent and obvious potential, Pastor McGovern could often be rude to people. He showed little patience when there were administrative glitches in the church. He treated the volunteer workers of the ministry who were not always as reliable as they could be much like a hard-driving boss in the corporate world. He was hard on Sunday School teachers who did not meet attendance goals. He was demanding on ushers and others who assisted in the ministry. He ran the church office like the business world. He would not return phone calls if the party who called was in his "dog house." He often would not see people who had not first made an appointment to see him. Though a gifted pulpiteer, behind the scenes he was hard to work with. "Prima donna" might be a term to describe his working

The Art of Pastoring

relationship with people. He was critical of any detail which was not right and let the person responsible know it.

The same tenor was evident in church board meetings. He pretty much ran roughshod over men who did not share his views. Needless to say, though he was talented, his ministry in that church was a rough ride. What went around, came around. People in positions of leadership came to respond in the tone set by Pastor McGovern. He faced a succession of splits, departures, and general unrest in the church. The dead fly of an insensitive spirit eventually fouled the ointment of his ministry.

8. **Finances** - As noted earlier, three things which can get a pastor into trouble in the ministry are money, morals, and malice. Let us consider the first of that triad. Jesus taught a parable of a man beginning a building program and then later finding out he did not have enough money to finish it. *"For which of you intending to build a tower, sitteth not down first, and counteth the cost, whether he hath sufficient to finish it,"* (Luke 14:28. It has been said about our Lord's earthly ministry, He had more to say about how we handle our money and how our money handles us than He did about the gospel. Money certainly was mentioned frequently in His ministry. The handling of money may not make a pastor, but it certainly has the potential to break him.

Though he may not have direct control of church finances, like any executive officer, he will be blamed for what takes place on his watch for better or for worse. Though the pastor usually is not the official financial controller of the church, in a practical way he certainly is the de facto controller. His influence will either encourage spending or encourage restraint. When finances get out of hand in a church, it may not be the pastor's fault. But invariably, he is blamed when the church gets in over its head financially. Though the pastor may not have spent the money himself, and though he may have had reservations about going into debt, by tacitly approving indebtedness, he becomes the lightning rod for blame if things go wrong.

Flies in the Ointment

Pastor Rukavina's church was in a growing community. Times were good, and the local economy was booming. Because there was rapid growth in the community, his church was growing as well. Companies had moved to town over the past decade, and the local population was constantly expanding. However, Pastor Rukavina interpreted the growth of his church to his leadership. Because there were many new people in the community without a church home, it was relatively easy to reach them. Pastor Rukavina did not link the expansion of the local economy and the population to the growth of his church. He linked the church growth to his preaching and programs. Therefore, in conjunction with the leadership of the church, he proposed a major building program. They assumed the growth of the church would continue as it had in recent years. Moreover, they took the risky position they could overbuild for anticipated growth because inflation would make it easier to repay their mortgage in coming years. Therefore, following Pastor Rukavina's leadership, the church voted to borrow a large sum. The debt service became a substantial percentage of their monthly budget, but times were good, and they were able to carry the load.

However, two years later, the national economy went into a serious recession. The dynamics of the downturn were amplified in the local economy. Numerous people in Pastor Rukavina's church were laid off. Two major plants in the community closed and transferred a large number of people to plants in other states. Dozens of families in the church moved away. The offerings of the church took a major drop. Suddenly, the church was in a financial crisis. Most of the church staff was laid off. Even then, the offerings could not support the debt service the church had incurred. Mortgage payments began to be in arrears. The financial institution which had loaned the church the money threatened to foreclose. Pastor Rukavina's ministry was in a major crisis. He had led the church into debt, but they were unable to pay for it. The church went through major restructuring, discouragement, and great stress. Finally, the building was sold to a charismatic group which was able to carry the

The Art of Pastoring

load. Pastor Rukavina was a broken man. He had began to build a tower but did not have the resources to finish it. The dead fly of unwise financial decisions had soured the ointment of his ministry.

* * *

Pastor Fedo pastored a church in a small community. He enjoyed the ministry and was well thought of by his church. He was a fairly good preacher and a good pastor to his people. However, Pastor Fedo was the kind of person who did not worry much about details. He often was careless about balancing his checkbook and got around to reconciling it with the bank perhaps once a year. There always was a major difference between his figures and that of the bank. He just didn't take the time or effort to keep on top of his personal finances. His wife often took care of family business, and he was happy to allow her to do it. They also carried credit card debt with a substantial balance. They usually only paid the minimum payment each month. They saved nothing.

Pastor Fedo was slipshod in his tithing. As he was careless in the rest of his financial affairs, he was careless in this regard as well. He managed to put a "tithe" check in the offering on a regular basis, but when things got tight, well, he figured he would make it up later. However, he only tithed on the "net" of his *salary* check. Not only did he ignore his federal and state withholding along with social security withheld, he also conveniently forgot the non-taxable portions of his compensation. He did not tithe on the value of his free use of the parsonage, appurtenances, and utilities provided by the church. Nor did he tithe on his auto allowance. He figured if it was tax deductible for the IRS, it must be tithe-exempt as well. Moreover, he forgot about the worth of the health policy the church carried for him and his family as well as his retirement fund. Therefore, his giving in proportion to his overall compensation package certainly did not come close to ten percent. It may have been six per cent at best, not including the times he forgot to place a check in the offering plate or could not. "Will a man rob God?"

He and his family had lived in the church parsonage for several years. However, it was old and not energy-efficient. Therefore, he talked the matter over with his deacons, and decided he would buy his own home. He didn't think much about how the use of the church parsonage was a significant part of his compensation package. He just assumed the church would raise his salary to match his house payments. The church agreed to sell the parsonage and use some of the proceeds to help Pastor Fedo buy his own home. He used that money for a down payment. The church, as agreed, gave him a housing allowance to help him with his house payments.

However, a series of events took place which Pastor Fedo had not anticipated. First, the church had a minor split which diminished the church budget some. The church could not pay him as much as they had anticipated. The actual housing allowance was by no means the equivalent to his mortgage payment, property taxes, utilities, insurance, and maintenance. Then, the sewer line at his house collapsed and had to be replaced all the way to the street. To his dismay, he learned his old sewer cut across his neighbor's property and the neighbor would not grant permission to cut down the trees in his yard to replace the sewer. The city therefore required him to run a new sewer down the alley at a considerably greater expense. He was forced to take a second mortgage to finance that. Suddenly, the cost of two mortgage payments, credit card bills, miscalculated checkbook balances, plus payments for the two cars and the camper he owned brought Pastor Fedo to a major crisis. He could not pay his bills. He tried to sell the camper but was offered only a fraction of what it was worth. The credit card companies had turned his accounts over to collection agencies. They threatened to place liens on his property. He had to let the bank repossess his second car. Still, he could not dig himself out of debt.

The people of the church by now were becoming aware of his troubles. Some felt sorry for their pastor and tried to help him individually with small gifts. Others, were embarrassed that the pastor of *their* church was such a poor business testimony in the community.

The Art of Pastoring

To receive protection from his creditors and their threats of legal action, Pastor Fedo declared bankruptcy. The local newspaper, as was their regular practice, published the public record of his bankruptcy. His testimony in that small community was ruined. He reluctantly resigned his church, moved, and tried to start over again in the ministry elsewhere. The dead fly of financial carelessness had deeply damaged his ministry.

    9. Family embarrassment - Samuel, in writing about Eli the high priest, made the comment how "*his sons made themselves vile and he restrained them not,*" (I Samuel 3:13). That, along with other compromise, was the undoing of Eli's ministry. Much could be said about the training of one's children. However, one of the qualifications for the office of pastor as defined by the Apostle Paul is "*one that ruleth well his own house, having his children in subjection with all gravity,*" (I Timothy 3:4). Indeed, if a pastor cannot properly lead his own family, how can anyone expect him to lead a church?

    Pastor Gore was an excellent preacher. He had built a good ministry in the church he had pastored for some years. The church had grown from virtual obscurity to some renown in that region. However, Pastor Gore had a hidden secret which most people did not know. He was inconsistent in a number of areas of his personal life. Though he would preach against vulgar TV and Hollywood from the pulpit, he was not above watching that sort of thing at home. He tried not to do it in front of his children, but they came to know what dad did after they went to bed. He preached Christian living from the pulpit, but he could get into some terrible arguments with his wife. The kids knew their dad preached faithfulness; however, when they went on vacation, they were unfaithful in attending church services. He preached against rock 'n roll music, but listened to contemporary Christian music.

    His sons had a tendency to be two-faced. They could put on the angel act, but when out of sight of Mom and Dad, the real side of

Flies in the Ointment

their character emerged. People in the church would come to Pastor Gore from time to time and report some incident concerning his sons. He would become indignant and tell the messenger in so many words to mind his own business. He could take care of his family. Beside, his children wouldn't do that sort of thing anyway. After a while, his sons caught on how they had old Dad fooled (or so they thought). As they began to go through their adolescent years, they became more and more emboldened in their sin. They violated the purity of several girls in the church youth group. Some were willing accomplices, but one went and bitterly complained to her father about the preacher's kids. He went to the pastor to protest. Pastor Gore told him he would take care of it. He never did. As his sons reached mid and late adolescence, they began to experiment with alcohol and tobacco. Most of the teens in the church youth group knew about it. A few told their parents. Again, several parents went to Pastor Gore about the stories their children were bringing home. He said, it was all a bunch of vicious gossip by others who were jealous.

He either would not believe or did not want to believe his sons were into such sin. At home, they could act so spiritual. They seemed to have so much interest in the church youth group. What pastor Gore would not face was the truth about his sons. For years he had endeavored to sweep the problems under the proverbial rug. However, that rug was becoming too lumpy to ignore. There was too much smoke for there to not be some fire. The people in the church pretty well knew what was going on, especially those who had young people. They loved their pastor, but things were getting to the point where it could no longer be ignored. Finally, all of the ugly allegations came out in one traumatic deacons' meeting. Pastor Gore once again vainly tried to dismiss the complaints as gossip, jealous teenagers, and girls vindictive about being spurned. But in his heart, he knew better. And the people knew better. His ministry there was over, and he knew it. He began looking for another place, and not long after, he resigned and went elsewhere. The dead fly of

The Art of Pastoring

inconsistency which unraveled the spiritual character of his children almost ruined his ministry.

10. Moral failure - Proverbs 6:32 says, *"Whoso committeth adultery with a woman . . . destroyeth his own soul."* Moral failure is a terrible pollution in the ministry today. It has ruined a large number of pastors and churches.

Pastor Harkin had had a bright and rising ministry. His people loved him. He was an eloquent young preacher. His church was growing. He was a handsome man with a magnetic personality. One day a woman in the church came to him for counsel. She was the attractive wife of one of the leaders of the church. She confided how her marriage was a mess, and she was very unhappy. Pastor Harkin made the foolish error of privately counseling the woman on an ongoing basis. As he listened to her tearful story, he genuinely felt compassion for her. For her part, because her pastor was so sympathetic and kind, she "loved" her pastor even more. Though he knew better, Pastor Harkin realized he was developing romantic feelings toward the woman. She would make a point to be her most feminine and attractive when coming for counseling. One thing led to another, and they began having an affair. Though they were never "caught" as such, Pastor Harkin was so smitten with a guilty conscience, he got up in the evening service one Sunday night and resigned on the spot. He would not tell anyone why, only that it was for personal reasons. However, in due season the sordid story did leak out. Pastor Harkin had ruined his ministry, his testimony, his marriage, and the confidence his church had in him. The dead flies of foolishness which led to immorality uttered fouled the ointment of his ministry. He had not planned to commit adultery. It was not initially on his mind. But he foolishly allowed himself (1) to counsel a woman alone. (2) He had allowed himself to become emotionally involved with her. (3) He had yielded to the lust of his flesh and the temptation to commit adultery when the opportunity arose. It destroyed his ministry.

Flies in the Ointment

There no doubt are other flies which cause the ointment of a pastor's ministry to stink. They often seem so little. It is so easy to rationalize such matters. But the little flies of sin, whatever their nature, can surely unravel the fabric of a pastor's ministry. In some other profession, some of these things might be tolerated. For a pastor who by the very nature of his office has the reputation for wisdom and honor, they are not. Be warned. Be wise. Beware.

Chapter Twelve -
Three Final Commands

*"But watch thou in all things, endure afflictions . . .
make full proof of thy ministry."*

The Apostle Paul's final spiritual imperatives for pastors. A significant part of this book has been tracing the imperatives in the New Testament which pertain to the ministry of a pastor. II Timothy 4 is the culmination of Paul's instructions to Timothy. Verse 5 contains the final *spiritual* imperatives of his writing. There are several other personal things Paul wrote such as urging Timothy to come soon, bringing John Mark, and bringing certain personal effects when coming. But verse 5 is the last of Paul's imperatives pertaining to the pastoral ministry. There actually are four imperatives there. However, we examined doing the work of an evangelist in an earlier chapter. Therefore, here, we will consider the three remaining pastoral imperatives.

Whereas most of the various imperatives considered thus far pertained primarily to what a pastor ought to be doing, these final three deal largely with a pastor's character. In this regard, we are not speaking of his integrity, morals, or convictions. Rather, the thought is of the temperament, grit, and discipline needed in the pastoral ministry. Though on the one hand, the following qualities to a certain degree are innate; to a greater degree, they can be learned and therefore developed. Hence, they are set forth by the Holy Spirit as imperatives - things we ought to be developing in our personal character. Let's consider each of these.

The First of the Last

"*But Watch thou in all things*" - The Holy Spirit moved Paul to use an interesting word here. The word translated "watch thou" is "nepho." Thayer's Greek-English Lexicon defines the word as "to be calm and collected in spirit; to be temperate, dispassionate, circumspect." It is more commonly translated as "sober" in the Authorized Version. As Paul wrote this young preacher, he described the temperament a pastor ought to have. Individuals have varying predispositions regarding their temperament. For some, a given area may be stronger than another. Nevertheless, the Holy Spirit set forth the proper temperament a pastor should have. If a man is weak in these areas, it is something upon which he must therefore work.

The sense of the word "nepho" does not particularly pertain to self-discipline regarding physical appetites. Rather, the focus is upon one's mind, spirit, and emotions. In other words, Paul instructed Timothy to be *disciplined internally*. This internal discipline is likely in three areas: (1) our emotions, (2) our attitudes, and (3) our mind. Let us further examine each of these.

1. Disciplined emotions - In II Timothy 2:24-25, Paul already developed this idea. Notice how he instructed Pastor Timothy, "*And the servant of the Lord must not strive; but be gentle unto all men, apt to teach, patient, in meekness instructing those that oppose themselves.*" You may recall in the previous chapter how one fly fouling the ointment of the ministry is a pastor losing his temper. To lose one's temper is demonstrating for all to see that one is not disciplined emotionally. God has indeed created our various emotions within us. However, they never ought to control us. Rather, we must control them. To paraphrase Solomon, there is a proper time for just about anything. However, there rarely is a proper place for the venting of negative emotions such as anger, hatred, vengeance, or contentious debate. Of all people, this is true for a pastor.

In using the metaphor of a servant, Paul clearly instructed how a pastor ought not *strive*. The word so translated (machomai) has the sense of fighting, quarrelling, or disputing. (Notice how the root in "machomai" is "macho.") It might be "macho" to unload on someone with whom you disagree. It might be macho to be pugnacious, not yielding in argument. And, for the world, that no doubt is true. However, the clear imperative for a pastor is how "the servant of the Lord must not strive." He must control the urge to be "macho."

Years ago, as a young man just beginning in the ministry, I witnessed a renowned pastor of great stature "lose his cool" over an incident. I was aghast. I certainly held this man in honor and reputation. My estimation of him was somewhat diminished thereafter. However, he, like everyone of us, had times when he succumbed to the temptation of losing his temper.

In the same passage, notice how Paul instructed Pastor Timothy to be "patient." There are several words in the Greek New Testament which are translated thus. In some cases, the thought is waiting or persevering in the face of difficulty. However, in other cases the thought is of putting up with people. That is the sense here. The word (anexikakos) has the sense of being patient with people. Once again, it pertains to the emotional disposition of a pastor. Anyone who has been in the ministry for any time knows there are people who for varying reasons can be annoying. In some cases, they don't know any better. In other cases, they need help. In some cases, they are just self-directed. They in one way or another demand a pastor's attention. Though a pastor may be sorely tempted to ignore them or be rude, we are enjoined to be patient with them. That requires emotional discipline. It is a part of a pastor's required temperament.

The Art of Pastoring

In a similar vein, Paul also noted how a pastor ought to be *meek* in dealing with troublesome people. The principle of meekness is most interesting. Contrary to popular misconception, meekness is not being timid, mousy, or a wimp. Rather, it bears directly upon a pastor's disposition, which we are discussing. The word so translated (prautes), according to W. E. Vine, has the sense of "a temperance of spirit," or "an equanimity of spirit." It practically speaks of one who is even-natured, has his emotions disciplined, does not "lose his cool," does not come "unglued," "get bent out of shape," or "lose it."

In most churches, there are people who are difficult to deal with. They are prickly. They are problems waiting to happen. Some cannot be noticed in any other forum of life, so they try to make a splash in the church. There are people who often are headed for disaster or failure in life. Their folly is obvious. Yet, they either do not have the faculties to change their lot or are not willing to do so. A pastor can see their trouble is the harvest of what they have sown. Still, they give the pastor and others in church leadership headaches. The irony is that while at times causing problems for the pastor, they in fact lurch headlong toward even greater chaos in their own life. This pastor has been sorely tempted on occasion to "read them the riot act." The urge is strong to tell them to get lost. "Take your self-inflicted problems and go elsewhere. You are a mess and the source of your own trouble!"

But a pastor cannot do that. The Scripture says, "*in meekness instructing those that oppose themselves*." We are charged to not only be patient in dealing with such troublesome people, but to do so in an even-natured way. We are obligated to try and help them with our emotions disciplined, not showing disgust, irritation, or lack of interest. God has placed us there to try and help them even when such help seems to be an exercise in futility. Unfortunately, if a pastor is rough and uses a hard line, they in turn may begin to peddle how cold-hearted, unloving, and uncompassionate he is. Those are hard charges to live down. We are charged to be disciplined in our emotions. In my father's years, I have no recollection of him ever dealing roughly with anyone. To the contrary, even those who were less than loyal later openly characterized him as a "prince" of a man. He was kind, courteous, and decent to all.

2. Disciplined attitudes - In like fashion, the apostle instructed Pastor Timothy to be "*gentle unto all men*" (literally, "gentle to all"). The word translated "gentle" is "epios." It has the sense of a mild or gentle attitude such as a mother working with her children or a teacher helping a student. Parents or teachers know children can at times be aggravating. Nevertheless, a position of leadership demands a fair, moderate, and patient attitude in working with them. It goes with the territory. It is part of the job description.

In the secular world, we all have noticed someone in a position of leadership whose deportment was odious. A rude, overbearing government official is not thought of well. However, an officer who is courteous, fair, and has a pleasant attitude is much easier to receive. So ought be the attitude of a pastor. Pastors who are not careful can obtain a poor reputation in the community. I am mindful of a pastor of a church of another denomination. The only thing we share in common is we happen to live in the same general community. This particular fellow presides over a high-profile church making waves in the community. However, in the business and professional world, he is thought of as a "jerk." Those who deal with him on a professional and business level consider him overbearing and pushy. Sooner or later, such a reputation will catch up with a man. Of all people, a pastor ought to be renowned as having a gentle attitude in dealing with people whether they are in his church or not.

Moreover, a pastor is charged to be "*apt to teach*." To be sure, a pastor ought to have the training, education and wherewithal to teach others the Word of God. Implicit is the matter of being prepared for a given message or class. However, the word the apostle used (didaktikos) implies not only skill in teaching, but also an attitude. That attitude is a willingness to teach. It is an attitude which views teaching others God's Word as a privilege rather than a burden. It implicitly describes a willing spirit in contrast to a foot-dragging spirit. There are countless ways and opportunities for a pastor to teach his people. They range from formal adult Sunday School or the pulpit to working with a wayward teenager. People quickly pick up on a pastor whose attitude concerning imparting God's Word is a burden. A key to having a receptive audience is a willing, excited attitude on the part of the pastor.

3. A Disciplined Life - As noted in the previous chapter, there are various "little" things which can effectively ruin the ministry of a pastor. A large proportion of those flies in the ointment are directly related to a lack of self-discipline in the various aspects of life. The people in the pew may get away with lack of temperance. A pastor will not. Paul in writing to the Corinthian church noted how *"Every man that striveth for the mastery is temperate in all things,"* (I Corinthians 9:25). The context of the passage is of a long-distance runner illustrating Christian self-discipline. It ultimately will be rewarded with an incorruptible victor's crown upon crossing the finish-line before the bema seat. If there ever were a spiritual application of that principle, it is in the pastoral ministry. For a man to master this special office, he *must* be self-disciplined. Anything less will result in shortcomings. The shortcomings then become the flies which cause the ointment of his ministry to stink.

In leading up to this principle, the apostle alludes to a marathon type of race. *"Know ye not that they which run in a race run all, but one receiveth the prize? So run that ye may obtain,"* (I Corinthians 9:24). This author lives in a city which conducts a world-class marathon each year along the shores of Lake Superior. Though runners come from around the world to run the race each summer, thousands of locals run the race as well. To run 26-plus miles requires a tremendous amount of personal discipline on the part of each runner. They *must* work out strenuously for many weeks preceding the big race. All over the city, even in the winter, people are seen running in preparation for the marathon race in June. They discipline their eating habits. They discipline their minds to resist pain. In the final hours before the race, they discipline their sleep. The day before the race, they discipline their calorie and carbohydrate intake. Most of all, much self-discipline is needed to finish the race. If the day is warm or the humidity high, finishing the race becomes an exercise in self-inflicted torture. I have stood along the race course and watched the lesser prepared runners struggle to keep going, their faces gaunt, their bodies being pushed to the limits of endurance. It is not uncommon for runners crossing the finish line to collapse. They knew they would not win the race, but their goal was to finish the course. They therefore disciplined their minds to endure the pain and just keep on going.

Disciplined to finish the course. In writing to Timothy, Paul reminded him how he had finished his course (II Timothy 4:7). That course was the marathon of the ministry God had given him. Reading the various divinely inspired accounts of Paul's life in Acts, Corinthians, and elsewhere, it is evident his course was not easy. But he possessed that spiritual discipline of body and mind which enabled him to finish.

The ministry in general and the pastoral ministry in particular require a man to be mentally and spiritually disciplined. Being faithful before the throne of grace in prayer requires a disciplined life. Having a systematic, consistent time in the Word of God *each day* requires self-discipline. Preparing proper messages in a timely fashion requires discipline to study at length *each week*. Taking care of administrative detail demands discipline and focus of mind. It is not a gift. It is work. It requires discipline for a man to do what he ought to do before he does what he wants to do. It takes discipline of schedule to consistently visit people either as a pastor or as a soul winner. It takes discipline of mind to maintain proper balance in financial matters both personally and of the church. To maintain a proper schedule, a man must be personally disciplined. Mastery of the office of pastor will never occur until a man is temperate in all things. There must be discipline of one's body. But even more, there must be a discipline of one's mind. An undisciplined man will never achieve mastery of a pastoral ministry. Moreover, he likely will fail therein altogether. The key to spiritual faithfulness, in a word, is discipline. The key to obeying the numerous imperatives pertaining to a pastoral ministry require discipline. It is not only an invisible secret to the ministry, it is a necessary ingredient.

A related principle is that of diligence. It is an interesting concept. If Paul is the author of Hebrews (of which position this author leans), he had something to say on the matter of diligence. In Hebrews 6:10-11, we read, *"For God is not unrighteous to forget your work and labour of love, which ye have shewed toward his name, in that ye have ministered to the saints, and do minister. And we desire that every one of you do shew the same diligence."* The word so translated, "spoude," or its verbal cousin "spoudadzo," both have the same essential idea. It is "to hasten the matter." Diligence is the opposite of procrastination. When it comes right down to it, it is a disciplining of one's life in regard to time. In all of the 50-plus years of my father's ministry, I cannot ever remember a time in which he was late. That is not to say it never happened. I just don't recall it. Dad was diligent. He was sensitive to the scheduling of his time as it related to other people. If someone made an appointment, he saw to it that they were not left waiting. He made it a point to not only be on time, but usually early. He loathed keeping someone waiting for him. He had respect to their time and its worth.

Diligence is a simple matter. It is discipling one's mind to keep track of time regarding whatever *ought* to be done. It is a simple outworking of the greater principle of righteousness. Henry Sorenson was diligent in the preparation of his messages. Never did he wait until Saturday night to come up with a message for Sunday morning. Never did he wait until the last minute to pay his bills. Never did he wait until the last minute to get something done which needed to be done. He impelled himself to discipline his time, schedule, and duties to do what *ought* to be done in a timely fashion. He well knew the possibility of an ox falling in a ditch disrupting his schedule.

Therefore, he always was prepared for Sunday well ahead of time. Diligence is a discipline of one's time so things are accomplished on time.

Talent or personality will never compensate for discipline. Discipline is independent of talent. Long-term success in the ministry requires more than being gifted. Talented people at times have a higher failure rate than more ordinary men. The reason is as simple as it is profound. They have relied upon their talent. However, talent will never be a substitute for the integrity of character which comes from the self-discipline to do as one ought to do.

Discipline is independent of personality. A charming, charismatic personality certainly can be a plus. But it is the nitty-gritty of the inward discipline of mind and spirit which enables us to finish the course God has set before us. The hare of charisma will never win the long-term race of the ministry. To the contrary, it usually is a casualty along the way. It is the tortoise of godly discipline which gets the job done. Being organized certainly is not glamorous or dynamic. But organization built upon godly discipline by God's Spirit will outlast a disorganized, undisciplined man regardless of how dynamic or talented he might be.

Discipline derives from righteousness. Discipline is the practical outworking of the more basic biblical principle of righteousness. On a practical level, righteousness is doing as we ought to do. It is the engine which pulls the train of Christian character. We will never do as we ought to do until we discipline ourselves to do what is right. Anything we truly ought to do is righteous. And conversely, if a matter is right, I therefore ought to do it. The transmission which links our real life to the intangible principle of righteousness is self-discipline. It disciplines us to do as we ought to do - that is, righteousness on a practical level.

Returning to the metaphor of a vehicle, if the transmission is slipping, the engine of righteousness can be revved up endlessly. However, its torque will never be effective until the transmission of discipline begins delivering that power to the wheels of day-to-day living. In Acts 24:25 is the account of how Paul stood before the Roman proconsul Felix and "*reasoned of righteousness, temperance, and judgment to come.*" The sequence of character traits there is not coincidental. Righteousness is the goal, but temperance is the means. Judgment to come is the result. It likewise is not coincidental how one of the final commands by Paul to his young protégé, Pastor Timothy, was a further development of the matter of personal discipline. It is necessary in a pastor's emotions, attitudes, and his life in general. It is the invisible secret to Christian character in general and the pastoral ministry in particular. It will be the invisible motivating force laying beneath the surface of the final two imperatives which Paul issued to Timothy.

The Second Command

"*Endure Afflictions*" - The next imperative in the final cluster of commands will ring true to any pastor who has been in the work for any length of time. The word translated "endure afflictions" (kakopatheo) has the sense "to endure trouble," or "to endure problems." If there is a calling in life which seems to attract problems, it is being a pastor. Few men long in the pastorate have not at one time contemplated quitting, or going elsewhere.

1. The ministry is one succession of problems. Problems come in all forms and ways. They at times seem insurmountable, especially those which are political in nature. Politics are people. The pastoral ministry is working with and dealing with people. As noted earlier in this book, a standing joke among pastors is how the ministry would be great, if it weren't for the people. The ministry of a New Testament church by its nature is political. There is an organizational structure made up of people. Some are cooperative; some are not; some are mature; some are not; some are spiritual; some are carnal. Some assume a church is run like a union and bring that sort of mentality into church matters. Some think a church is operated like the board of directors of a secular corporation. They often have a "board-run" mentality.

A pastor can come away from a deacons' meeting with his stomach literally churning. He may stay awake most of the night agitated over statements made in a committee meeting. Because a pastor's position in a Baptist church is by election of the congregation, that position to some extent is political. There is no pastor who has not wondered where he stood in the minds of his congregation. Those who have pastored for any length of time will swiftly pick up how the loyalty of people can suddenly change. Those whom a pastor *thought* were loyal backers of his ministry one day are undercutting it the next. Even if he does not have overt evidence to that end, he often can see it in the eyes of people. They get "that look." They are not with him any more. He does not know if they are going to leave the church, possibly taking others with them, or if they may try to start an undercurrent to unseat him. There are the business meetings which a pastor knows can take unpredicted and unpleasant twists. These things and more can give a pastor the desire to flee. Some burn out of the ministry all together. Most just look for another place.

The Apostle Paul wrote to Pastor Timothy, "Endure afflictions." It is the same word and same sense when he wrote, "*Thou therefore endure hardness, as a good soldier of Jesus Christ,*" (II Timothy 2:3). A soldier in battle will face many problems, not the least the enemy trying to kill him. A pastor will not likely face that problem. However, the principle is the same. Soldiers are tempted to go AWOL, to flee the battle, to run. Pastors face the same temptation. Though Paul was never a long-term pastor, he saw enough of the local church ministry to know Timothy (and all other New Testament pastors following him) would face problems in the ministry. Therefore, he urged Timothy to endure those problems. Ride them out. Keep on keeping on!

2. The ministry is one succession of pressures. In addition to political problems which may build, there are other things which make for stress. Fortunate is the pastor who does not have concerns about church finances. Usually, there is the mortgage to pay, missionary commitments which have been made, staff people depending upon the church for their livelihood, and all the rest of the items in a church budget. Even the best of churches face times of financial stress. It may be external, economic dynamics such as layoffs or people being transferred. It may be borrowing or spending which has been overly ambitious. It may be unexpected problems in the church building which places stress on church resources. It all comes back to the pastor. Though a board or committee might in theory be responsible, the real pressure is always on the pastor.

There may come pressure of doctrinal under-currents in the church. In the day of modern multi-media, people in the church get a hold of tapes, books, or other sources of theological material which enamors them. They begin to espouse a position which is not altogether synchronous with the historic position of the church and the pastor. Few deacons will lose sleep over such matters, but the pastor may. He is the overseer, especially of areas which pertain to doctrine. Others in the church are influenced by the ministries of TV preachers and their compromise. They put pressure on the pastor to attend or support certain conferences. Or, they simply exert pressure to adopt a less biblical position in areas of separation. They want the church to invite college groups with which the pastor is not at ease. They want their church to be like Dr. So and so's. They are influenced by the modern fads of the ministry. They see other "progressive" churches adopting such "reforms." Why is their pastor so obstinate in resisting change?

These pressures can cause a pastor to literally develop ulcers, high blood pressure, and even heart trouble. To the average layman in the church, they don't seem like that big a deal, but to a conscientious pastor, there is real stress in such issues. Paul counseled, "Endure afflictions."

3. **The ministry is also one succession of prodigals**. People may not cause a pastor trouble or overt stress, but they can certainly

disappoint him to the point of discouragement. The pastor has the blessing of seeing a family come to Christ through his ministry. Through either his direct ministry or that of others in the church, he has the joy of watching them grow in the Lord. They seemingly are genuinely discipled. They seem to be growing in grace. They becomes friends and develop a bond of fellowship. But then one day, they slip back into the world. They may have the character to call the pastor and tell him they are going back to "their" old church. More often, they simply disappear. No amount of visits, prayer, or contacts makes any difference. They just up and quit, sometimes going deeply into the world and sin. It breaks the pastor's heart. He has prayed for them, worked with them, taught them, and poured his heart into them. Their forsaking of him, having loved this present world is a discouragement.

Maybe the scenario is not so drastic. After having been saved through the ministry of the church or the pastor himself, a young couple grows and begins to blossom spiritually. They have great potential, and the pastor knows it. They are such an asset to the church. The pastor is so proud of them. They have become valuable workers in the church. Then one day comes the phone call. They are moving to a distant state. All of the spiritual work and effort in discipling them seems to be of nought in so far as that church is concerned. It is discouraging.

Then there is the frequent disappointment of seeing young people who have grown up in the church kick over the traces and head for the world. In their grade school years, they were so sweet and cooperative. Their junior high years were cute in their awkwardness. They seemed to be dedicated as high school students. Then upon graduating from high school or not long after, they make a swan-dive into sin and the world. They become promiscuous, hitting the world's night spots, neutralizing all their godly training in degenerate living. It happens all the time. Their parents are crushed, and the news is discouraging to a pastor. It seems all his efforts to train the young people in his church have come to nought.

The Art of Pastoring

The counsel of the apostle remains the same, "Endure afflictions." Whether the "afflictions" are problems, pressures, or prodigals, they are very real in the pastoral ministry. Every man who has pastored any length of time knows full well of these troubles and more. The standing command for every pastor of a New Testament church has not changed.

The Final Command

Make full proof of thy ministry - The final imperative pertaining to the ministry by Paul to Timothy was direct. "*Make full proof of thy ministry.*" The word translated "make full proof" is "pleophoreo." It has an expanse of thought ranging from "fulfill," to "carrying through to the end," to "accomplishing the task." The several former thoughts are probably what is in view in light of the context. In other words, Paul admonished Timothy to fulfill his ministry, to accomplish it completely, to carry it through to the end, to not quit, to not drop out.

Once again, the long distance race comes into view. It often is not easy. The scenery of the ministerial landscape is littered with many a man who started out in the ministry, but for one reason or another did not finish the course. It may have been any one of a number of flies which fouled the ointment of their ministry. However, sometimes the case is men who found the marathon of a life-long pastoral ministry something they could not or would not complete. Like John Mark in his early ministry, when the going got tough, they just quit. John Mark had travelled with Paul on part of his first missionary journey. The opposition and hardships of first-century missionary work did not turn out to be the romantic ministry he may have envisioned. Therefore, after facing opposition on Cyprus, upon arriving back on the mainland at Pamphylia, John Mark up and quit. This author has witnessed numerous peers who started the race decades ago, but no longer are in the battle. For whatever reason, they dropped out. Like the unprepared marathon runner, the race became too much for them.

In a similar vein, the author of Hebrews wrote to wavering brethren, *"Wherefore seeing we also are compassed about with so great a cloud of witnesses, let us lay aside every weight, and the sin which doth so easily beset us, and let us run with patience the race that is set before us, looking unto Jesus the author and finisher of our faith; who for the joy that was set before him endured the cross, despising the shame, and is set down at the right hand of the throne of God,* (Hebrews 12:1-2). The context is of wavering Hebrew brethren contemplating returning to Judaism. However, the parallels to the ministry are compelling. The witnesses mentioned probably are the great olympic stadium of saints who have already crossed the finish line noted in Chapter 11. In that heavenly throng are many a pastor who in all likelihood endured much greater difficulties than a modern American pastor. The author, therefore, urges his readers to likewise (1) lay aside the weights which hinder one from finishing the race. (2) Jettison the sin which easily besets (i.e., stop breaking the rules lest one be disqualified). There is a race to finish. And then, (3) run with patience the race set before us. The word translated "patience" is "hupomone" which in this context essentially has the sense of perseverance. Just keep on keeping on.

Set your sights on the finish line and He who is waiting there. Look unto Jesus. All of the difficulties, discouragements, and problems can powerfully tempt one to quit if they are the focus. Rather, we are admonished to take the focus off our troubles and turn our eyes upon Jesus. Moreover, He endured the race. He finished His course. He, for the joy that was set before Him, endured the cross, despising the shame and is now set down at the right hand of the throne of God. Though none of us as pastors will ever merit that privilege, hopefully we can look forward to the crown of glory which fadeth not away which He has promised to those who have faithfully served as pastors. The point the author of Hebrews is driving at is that Jesus endured the cross. He finished His course. He did not give up. If He could endure such "contradiction of sinners" which we will never face, is it too much to expect us to finish our course? He did it. He set the example. He is there waiting at the finish line urging us on. He in effect is there saying, "I did it! I made it! You can too. Don't give up! Keep on running. You can make it!"

The Apostle Paul made the comment how *"the gifts and calling of God are without repentance,"* (Romans 11:29). When God calls a man into the ministry, he doesn't uncall him ten years later. It is a call for life. Therefore, as Pastor Timothy, we are enjoined to make full proof of our ministry.

Henry Sorenson began preaching as a young deacon before he ever went to Bible college. He kept right on even after age demanded he retire. In retirement, he jumped at the chance to remain in the gospel ministry as an assistant pastor. Though he had officially finished his course, he continued to make full proof of his ministry. He did so up until the day he went to heaven. He was still preaching, teaching, visiting, and winning people to Christ. Even on his final hospital bed, he won people to Christ. He had fought a good fight. He had finished his course. He had kept the faith. Henceforth, there no doubt is laid up for him a crown of righteousness, which the Lord, the righteous judge, shall give him at that day. He had not only fed the flock of God, but faithfully pastored it as an ensample to the flock. He therefore also will no doubt receive a crown of glory that fadeth not away. I trust each young pastor or those aspiring to pastor will likewise seek and achieve those crowns as well.

"The Lord Jesus Christ be with thy spirit. Grace be with you. Amen."

Appendix

(1.) Our focus throughout this book has been upon the office of the pastor. However, let us briefly take note of the five gifts mentioned in Ephesians 4:11. The first two, apostles and prophets were temporary gifts to the tender, young church of the first century. The office of apostle was limited to those who were directly chosen and sent by Jesus Christ. The word "apostolos" literally means a 'sent messenger.' Such an one was sent with a specific message. In the New Testament, our Lord specifically chose and sent twelve apostles. In addition, each of them were eyewitnesses to His resurrection. (The term is also used in a broader sense to refer to other preachers such as Barnabas, Silvanus, and Timothy. However, with regard to these, the term is used generically and does not refer to them holding the actual office of apostle.) As each of the apostles died, their respective office died with them. It was not transferable. When the last of the apostles expired, perhaps in A.D. 96, the office and gift of apostle died with him. It was given by Jesus Christ to the fledgling church to strengthen and help it take root downward.

The office of prophet in the early church was temporary as well, but for a different reason. Like their counterparts in the Old Testament, prophets both forth-told as well as foretold the Word of God. They were preachers. However, the distinction between a preacher today and the office of prophet then is the source of his truth. Today, a biblical preacher will derive his authority and message from the Bible. However, in the church of the first century, for the most part, there was no New Testament. It either had not been written or its writing was incomplete and very limited in its propagation. Therefore, God gave a number of special, interim, and temporary gifts to individuals within local churches. These gifts, as noted in I Corinthians 12, were all supernatural in nature. They were given through the agency of the Holy Spirit to help, strengthen, guide, verify, and authenticate the fledgling church in the absence of a completed New Testament.

One of those gifts was that of prophecy (I Corinthians 12:10, and 12:28). To the New Testament prophet, the Holy Spirit directly revealed truth which would soon be available through the written New Testament. The source of his authority and message was by direct revelation. To the various local churches scattered across the first century, God gave prophets as a "medium" of revealing His truth. However, as the New Testament was completed and propagated, the interim gift of prophecy faded away. In I Corinthians 13:9, Paul wrote that prophecies would fail, and that the gift of prophecy was merely in part (partial). As the first century neared its culmination, the final book of the New Testament in the Revelation of John was completed. With it faded the office of the prophet. It today is extinct and has been since that time

The other gifts mentioned remain active to the present. Paul noted the office of evangelist. As the term suggests, this office is primarily fulfilled in evangelizing. That is, it is winning people to Christ. A modern error is how God bestows upon various people within a church "the gift of evangelism." These supposedly are the soul winners in a church. The rationale is that some have this gift and some don't. Therefore, if one does not have the gift of evangelism, it is not incumbent upon him to actively seek to win people to Christ. However, the truth of the matter is, evangelism is a command and not a gift. We all are called to witness and endeavor to win people to Christ. In the New Testament, beginning with the Great Commission given in Matthew 28 and onward, the matter of evangelism is presented as a comprehensive command in at least ten places. All Christians are under this imperative of Jesus Christ to evangelize others.

However, God has nevertheless given men to the church who have been called to a specific ministry of evangelism. As the term implies, their ministry is to evangelize by public preaching or personal witness. Philip is noted as the first official evangelist in Acts 21:8. Evangelists remain a gift to the church to strengthen, encourage, and revive through preaching and the winning of the lost. It is a unique gift from Christ to the church and it remains active to this day.

(2.) Six different words were used in the Greek New Testament by the Holy Spirit which are translated "feed" in the Authorized Version. Of the six, "poimaino" is the weakest in regards to the idea of feeding. Its only relationship thereto is by extension and implication from the primary idea how a shepherd among other things will be concerned with the food of his flock. The other five words translated "feed" are all much stronger regarding feeding.

(3.) As is the case of the term "elder," the term "pastor" has its background in the Old Testament. In the familiar twenty-third Psalm, the Lord is called our Shepherd. In fashion similar to the sense of the New Testament, the Hebrew word at times translated as "feed" ("ra-ah") may also be translated as "to shepherd" or "to pastor." Therefore, in Isaiah 40:11 the prophet wrote, *"He shall feed his flock like a shepherd: he shall gather the lambs with his arm, and carry them in his bosom, and shall gently lead those that are with young."* The context is of the Lord carefully taking care of His sheep. The word "ra-ah" (translated "feed") may be translated as "pastor." On eight occasions in the Old Testament, the spiritual leaders of God's people were referred to as "pastors." Again, the word so translated is "ra-ah" which is the basic word for shepherd (i.e. Psalm 23:1).

(4.) As noted in Chapter 2, the Hebrew word "raw-ah" (translated as "feed") is similar in nature to the Greek word "poimen" (or its verbal form, "poimano"). It fundamentally means "to shepherd." Moreover, there is a considerable interplay of words in the Hebrew text not obvious in the Authorized Version. The word translated "shepherd" in verse 2 is a qal active participle of "raw-ah." In *every case* except two in the Old Testament where the word "shepherd" appears in the Authorized Version, it is translated from the qal active participle of "raw-ah" (i.e., one shepherding). Its basic sense is to shepherd. In eight places, it is translated as "pastor."

However, the *same word* is used twice later in Ezekiel 34:2 where it is translated "feed." In the first case it even is the same conjugation (qal active participle). The point is, the word "raw-ah" most definitely means "to shepherd." A different word is used for the word "fed" in verse 3 (baw-ree).

About the Author

David Sorenson is a third generation, fundamental, Baptist pastor. He grew up in the home of Dr. Henry C. Sorenson who pastored for 55 years. The author was born in Stillwater, Minnesota, where his father pastored what at that time was called the First Baptist Church of Stillwater. Henry Sorenson during those years was instrumental in leading that church out of the liberal American Baptist Convention. The Henry Sorenson family then moved to St. Cloud, Minnesota, where Dr. Sorenson became the pastor of the First Baptist Church for the next five years. Then, in 1958, Henry Sorenson accepted the call as pastor of the Faith Baptist Church of Pekin, Illinois. He pastored there for the next 31 years where he retired in 1989.

His son, David Sorenson, who authored this book fought God's working in his life during his teenage years. However, in 1965, God got a hold of his life and directed him to attend Pillsbury Baptist Bible College in Owatonna, Minnesota. There he studied under the leadership of the late Dr. B. Myron Cedarholm. It was also there David Sorenson was born again. While a student at Pillsbury College, God called him into the gospel ministry.

Upon graduating from Pillsbury, God providentially directed him to enroll at Central Baptist Theological Seminary of Minneapolis under the leadership of the late Dr. Richard V. Clearwaters. While as a student working his way through seminary, he was asked to be a student intern pastor at Fourth Baptist Church and then an assistant pastor.

Upon graduating from seminary, David became the assistant and then associate pastor of Faith Baptist Church in Pekin, Illinois, working with his father for 10 years. He then became the senior pastor of First Baptist Church of Brainerd, Minnesota followed by a pastorate at the Sara Bay Baptist Church in Bradenton, Florida. While there, God led him to resign and return to Minnesota to start what became the Northstar Baptist Church in Duluth, Minnesota where he continues as pastor. At the time of this writing he is completing his Doctor of Ministry degree through Pensacola Christian College.

Additional Copies of this book
may be obtained from

Northstar Ministries
1315 South Arlington Avenue
Duluth, MN 55811
218-726-0209